God's *grace* in its various forms. —1 PET[...]

...sh and made his dwelling among us. We have seen his glory, the glory of the One and

...r my life worth nothing to me, if only I may finish the race and complete the task the Lord

...I commit you to God and to the word of his *grace*, which can build you up and

...r master, because you are not under law, but under *grace*. —ROMANS 6:14 ～ If by

...*e*. —ROMANS 11:6 ～ *grace* and peace to you from God our Father and the Lord

...*ace* to me was not without effect. No, I worked harder than all of them—yet not I, but

...that the *grace* that is reaching more and more people may cause thanksgiving to

...speech, in knowledge, in complete earnestness and in your love for us—see that you also

...fficient for you, for my power is made perfect in weakness." Therefore I will boast all the

～ It is by *grace* you have been saved, through faith—and this not from yourselves,

...been doing among you since the day you heard it and understood God's *grace*

...heirs having the hope of eternal life. —TITUS 3:7 ～ Let us then approach the throne of

...our time of need. —HEBREWS 4:16 ～ *grace* be with you all. —HEBREWS 13:25 ～

work in progress

work *in* progress

An Unfinished Woman's
GUIDE TO GRACE

Kristin Armstrong

New York   Boston   Nashville

All Scripture quotations are taken from the HOLY BIBLE:
NEW INTERNATIONAL VERSION. Copyright © 1973,
1978, 1984 by International Bible Society.
Used by permission of Zondervan Publishing House.

Some materials © 2008 by *Runner's World*. All rights reserved.
Published with permission of RODALE INC., Emmaus, PA.

FaithWords
Hachette Book Group
237 Park Avenue
New York, NY 10017

Visit our Web site at www.faithwords.com.

Printed in the United States of America

First Edition: March 2009
10 9 8 7 6 5 4 3 2 1

FaithWords is a division of Hachette Book Group, Inc.
The FaithWords name and logo are trademarks of
the Hachette Book Group, Inc.

Library of Congress Cataloging-in-Publication Data

Armstrong, Kristin.
    Work in progress : an unfinished woman's guide to grace / Kristin
Armstrong. — 1st ed.
        p.   cm.
    ISBN-13: 978-0-446-19800-4
    1. Christian women—Religious life.   I. Title.
    BV4527.A74 2009
    248.8'43—dc22

                                                              2008037865

Acknowledgments

$\mathcal{A}$ heartfelt thank you to the good people at Hachette—Meredith Smith, Rolf Zettersten, and Jana Burson. You make work fun and help refine me as I go/grow along.

Thank you to all my girlfriends who share their lives and their love. This book would not be what it is without you, nor would I. You know who you are. I love you.

Thank you, Mom, Dad, and Jon, for covering for me so I can run and write and breathe. Your support and unwavering confidence in me are true gifts. I love you.

Thank you, Luke, Grace, and Bella, for being such fine motivation to become a better woman. My heart is yours.

Contents

work in progress

Introduction

You may have met, or know, a woman like this: She brightens a room, can literally alter the energy before she opens her mouth. Her presence alone is uplifting, her warmth is genuine radiance, and her eye contact feels like a gift. Her compassion and confidence are unshakable. She knows herself well enough to be able to get to know you. She has no pretense about herself, has no need to hide because she lives in truth. She has no need to exalt or deprecate others or herself, and this allows others the freedom to be authentic in her company.

She is the kind of woman who makes you check your posture, inside and out. She makes you want to think before you speak, not because you feel judged or compelled to impress her, but simply because she makes you want to be better. Her integrity draws others into the light. Her laughter is contagious. Her hugs feel so good you wonder how you can get another one without appearing needy. When she is happy, you want to celebrate with her. When she is struggling, you want to stand by her side. Come to think of it, anything with her would be just fine.

Who is this woman? To me, she is a woman of grace.

And she is the reason I am writing this book. Not because I am a woman like this. I am a flawed woman . . . I spend too much at Target, I get very sour and sassy when I have PMS, I don't always pick up my dog's poop on a walk, I think new eye cream is a solution, I have eyed the clock in anticipation of a nice glass of red wine, I shush my children when I'm on the phone, I have memorized more song lyrics than Scripture, I have, in the past, cheered myself up with a new handbag. My spiritual walk has taken unnecessary side treks (off-road), and I have said and done things that I wish I could inhale and undo. I am as full of holes as I am good intentions.

But you know what? I know I can do better. I know that

with God's grace I can become a more graceful woman. I know I can do a better job of making Him proud, making Him happy He created me, or at least making Him laugh. Just like my children enjoy exceeding my expectations, I want to be a delight to my Creator.

I have some awesome, like-minded girlfriends, many of whom you will come to know while reading this book. They, like me, are open to improvement. We run marathons together, we have weekly track workouts followed by Bible study together, and we raise our children together. We're fortunate to be blessed by friendships like these. The idea for this book came about in conversation on about mile five of a twenty-mile run. We were discussing the hunger we had for improvement, for direction, and for companionship on our spiritual journeys. We believe these desires come from God. Acts 11:23 says, "When he arrived and saw the evidence of the grace of God, he was glad and encouraged them all to remain true to the Lord with all their hearts." When He arrives, I want Him to see evidence of grace — in me, in you, in all of us. We need to encourage one another.

I eagerly read *The Girlfriends' Guide to Pregnancy* by

Vicki Iovine when I was pregnant. And when I was in the pit of my divorce, I eagerly read every spiritual book and devotional I could get my hands on. Why? Because I wanted to connect with someone who knew exactly where I was and how I felt. And now at a time when society gives all kinds of wrong images about what it means to be a woman, I want to counteract the counterfeit by putting another message out there. I want to investigate what God has to say about what it means to be a woman. Not just any woman, but a graceful woman. I turned thirty-seven this year (that's over halfway to seventy, mind you), and I think it's time to find out.

Join me. I have chosen twelve traits of grace to explore. It's my hope that we emerge as more graceful women.

Kristin

ONE

Beauty

I used to be one of those women whose list of New Year's resolutions included items like: lose five pounds (or ten), drink more water, eat more protein, eat fewer carbs, exercise five times a week, purge closet and get rid of ugly clothes, drink wine only once a week, drink less coffee, do yoga, stretch more. My list looked more like a diary entry from Bridget Jones than a statement of goals and directions for Kristin Armstrong. Why? I don't have a weight problem. I guess wasting time by focusing on items like these is more indicative of a vanity problem or of misguided social conditioning. Perhaps I was confused about beauty, thinking that the harder I worked at it, the more diligent I became; or the more I deprived myself, this would somehow equate to greater beauty.

My first point of confusion was interpreting beauty as something to be aspired to instead of a reflection of who we are. From the time we are little girls we aspire to be women of beauty. To say that you have never once cared about this is to *lie, lie, lie*. We all want to be beautiful. But is it right to *aspire* to be beautiful? According to *Merriam-Webster's Dictionary*, the word *aspire* comes from the Latin word *aspirare*, which means "to breathe." This tells me something huge. We cannot strive our way into being beautiful. We have to relax into it; we need to breathe.

The world has unreliable standards. Throughout history the definition of beauty has shifted to reflect the mind-set and trends of the current society. Sometimes we should be curvy, other times rail thin; sometimes tanned, sometimes pale; sometimes with long hair, sometimes short hair, permed hair, straight hair, feathered hair (God help us); bright red lipstick, pale gloss; long acrylic nails, short real nails . . . All right already—I'm tired just typing this. We devote our energies to meeting the latest standard or at least reaching some approximation of it, and we are rewarded by . . . guess what? Another new mandate to chase after. It's an empty and relentless pursuit. Thank God we have another place to look for standards that are worthwhile and unchanging. *Up*.

God created each one of us specifically and beautifully. Among all of God's creation, we are the pinnacle, the icing on the cake, the signature on the masterpiece. This means that beauty is innate in each one of us in a way that is timeless and unalterable. Why are we wasting our time creating something that already exists within us? We can't. So what can we do instead?

We can unveil it.

Taking Off the Old

When it comes to beauty, each one of us carries baggage from childhood. Seemingly innocuous moments of our girlhoods are etched into our psyches with a Sharpie pen.

(And those really are permanent; remind me to show you my hallway upstairs.) I can remember some of mine, like changing for PE class in sixth grade and figuring out why all the boys loved this girl named Michele. Her body and my body looked like two different species. I changed in the bathroom after that. Or when I was putting on eyeliner in the crowded cafeteria bathroom mirror in eighth grade, and a girl named Tracey said, "That won't help you." Or this bossy boy in fourth grade who always picked me last for teams, saying, "She *sucks* in sports." (Do I? Six marathons later? But that "fact" about myself kept me on the sidelines until I was thirty-two.) You see? These moments, either painful or dismissive or both, are messages (lies, actually) spoken to our fragile images as we tentatively try to define who we are. I challenge us to understand that just as we didn't create ourselves, we do not have the power to define ourselves (and neither does anyone else). Only God can tell us who we are. But before we are ready to hear what He has to say about us, we have to do a little housecleaning (I probably need Tilex—how about you?) to remove the debris of old, untrue notions about ourselves and our beauty.

For a little spiritual Tilex on the mildew of our past, let's try 2 Corinthians 5:17: "If anyone is in Christ, he is a new creation; the old has gone, the new has come!" This verse is so powerful in combating the lies in our heads about our existence and our appearance. It is a Magic Eraser on the past, clearing our slates and removing the misperceptions and misplaced values imposed by ourselves or others. When we take off the old and realize that many "truths" we have built upon are actually false, spoken by voices other than God's, we begin to wake up.

Awake, awake, O Zion, clothe yourself with strength. . . . Shake off your dust; rise up, sit enthroned, O Jerusalem. Free yourself from the chains on your neck, O captive Daughter of Zion.

—Isaiah 52:1–2

We must pray for God to reveal those things that prevent us from seeing our true beauty. We must ask God to show us who we are and what we look like to Him. Though metaphorical for us, just like when Ananias cured Saul's blindness, we must remove the scales from our eyes.

~

Immediately, something like scales fell from Saul's eyes, and he could see again. He got up and was baptized.

—ACTS 9:18

~

We will never learn about beauty by looking at beauty magazines and comparing ourselves to airbrushed objects of so-called perfection. We are real women, in real relationships, doing real work, and our beauty is actively unveiled here, not captured in frozen poses. There is no comparison! I don't subscribe to any of those magazines anymore because if I did, I might begin to subscribe to them internally, and that is not acceptable to me. I have twin daughters, Grace and Bella, and those images are not what I want on our coffee table, permeating their young spirits and providing counterfeit standards. No, thank you!

Being a writer, I default to journaling when I have spiritual or inner work to do. Try it. Make a list of all the lies you have been told or have told yourself about who you are, what you look like, and what you are capable of. Pray 2 Corinthians 5:17 over every statement on your list. Then cross them out. *Yeah, baby.*

Putting on the New

Once we have prayed our way through clearing the old image rubble, we have more freedom to consider something new. When I say new, I don't mean that we suddenly look in the mirror (with scale-free, crow's-feet-free eyes) and see this glam girl winking coyly back at us. No. I mean an entirely new way of looking at ourselves that may, in fact, not include a mirror at all.

❧

See, I am doing a new thing! Now it springs up; do you not perceive it?

—Isaiah 43:19

❧

Just like taking off the old requires a detour through the past, so does putting on the new. Because our new is really not new, it is innate in who we are and has been part of our passion, purpose, and pleasure since our first breath. Think of what you loved to do when you were a child. I loved to fling myself as high as possible on the playground swing set, legs pumping, heart racing, head dizzy. Go back far enough in your memory that you can connect with the activity that made you lose sense of time and place and forget your skin and all your self-consciousness, so immersed were you in the moment of living your delight.

I loved to chase the waves on the beach for hours in my

Wonder Woman bathing suit, my braids filled with sand and my freckles multiplying in the squinting sun. I loved to run as fast as possible across the grass, thinking that if I could just get a little more speed, surely I would take off and fly. My parents told me that I could be anything I wanted to be when I was all grown up. "Anything?" I challenged. "Absolutely anything, honey," they replied.

"Okay, I want to be an eagle."

Just as the reality of Santa Claus and the Tooth Fairy eventually spoils the fun, I learned that I had to remain human, much to my dismay. However, this does not change the fact that there is a tiny place inside me that still feels like I was meant to fly, maybe not meant to be eternally tethered by my humanity. When that tiny place stirs, I can feel my feathers.

What gives you so much happiness that you do not give a second thought to how you look doing it? At mile twenty-five of a marathon, do you think I care that I am wheezing like a dying cow, gimping along with cramping calf muscles, covered in a whitewash of dried sweat scum, and smell like a locker room? No way; I am living a dream, face-to-face with my weakness, on the brink of de-spair, pushing past every fear of failure and success, totally humbled, totally lifted, totally exhausted, totally invigo-rated, and totally alive.

For my friend Paige, her thing is riding bareback on a horse, flying at top speed across the pasture, hair stream-ing out behind her, screaming "Yeeeee-hawwwwww" at the top of her lungs. For my friend KT, it is the trained, timeless, ageless way her body propels through water in the lanes at Deep Eddy pool. For my friend Jena, it is the weightless, bounding joy of her trampoline. For Laura, it is riding her bike and taking her hands and feet off the handlebars and pedals while coasting downhill. For Eliz-abeth, it's connecting with her inner gladiator, competing ruthlessly on the soccer field and doing a victory dance with every goal (or is it her compulsion to wrench a micro-phone from any performer onstage and belt out a tune of her own?). Jennifer cannot deny her internal ballerina as her feet inadvertently assume ballet positions while we do bicep curls in the gym mirror. Crystal cannot imagine life without sandy, sweaty beach volleyball. My friend Janie is a black belt. Who knew? Peggy can sew, knit, cook, or create anything, at any time. When I'm writing and I'm on a roll, I forget to eat—and I am someone who has to snack every two hours or I have a mood plummet of space shuttle proportions. What is it for you? What makes you lose track of your age, your decorum, the passage of time, or any constraint? What makes you feel like a kid?

Your assignment: travel down memory lane and re-claim your lost belongings.

If you honestly cannot remember, this is serious. Time for an intervention conversation with your mom, your sibling, or your oldest, bestest friend—because she will remember. Because it is that thing, the memory and the reacquaintance with it, that will clue you in to your beauty. When you are reveling in your passion and living your purpose, you are becoming transparent, reflecting the inner beauty of God. Think about it, when you watch someone doing the thing they were meant to do, aren't they gorgeous?

Well, so are you.

New Eyes

~

Give me your heart and let your eyes keep to my ways.

—Proverbs 23:26

~

Beauty is not about a reflection in a mirror. It is something God created, the essence of God Himself, and it stems from the heart. Changes in our appreciation for beauty need to come from the heart, not from the way we see ourselves with our eyes. In the verse above from Proverbs, God is asking us to relinquish our hearts to Him. He is the only One who can undo the damage that has been done to our hearts and heal us in such a way that we will have true vision. We have to believe that He can restore and reveal us.

He touched their eyes and said, "According to your faith will it be done to you."

—MATTHEW 9:29

When I went to a retreat called "Captivating," led by Stasi Eldredge, Stasi told us that each one of us has a special name given to us by God. It is something highly personal, incredibly intimate, and if you want to know what it is, ask God and He will reveal it to you. (I will admit, I was highly suspect.) I thought there was no way that the Creator of the universe would have the time or inclination to make up a pet name for me. Nicknames are cool, usually funny and based in love, indicative of close relationship. I figured that Stasi would get a special name, but I might just be Kristin Cate Richard Armstrong, or perhaps an assigned number. Like maybe God has a highly evolved Dewey decimal system to keep track of His flock, noting each one of us by a birth or death date and exact time. Doubting, but a direction-follower, I went outside for a covenant of silence, purportedly to speak to God about my so-called name.

I wasn't getting much in terms of two-way conversation with the Master, and I was starting to get cold, so I pulled my jacket over me like a blanket and lay down on top of the picnic table. I closed my eyes and turned my face toward the sun. Suddenly, out of nowhere, I got a visual of this time I went for a magical run with my best friend Paige, through these picturesque fields in Provence. We ran beside rows of lavender and endless miles of sunflowers. I remember feeling perfectly inserted in a postcard image, totally blessed, totally at home even in a foreign land. *Sunflowers . . . I have always loved the way they turn and follow the sun. Follow the sun, follow the Son; oh, dear God, yes! That's me. That's it. How many times have You given me sunflowers? OHMY-GOD (Sir), are you kidding me? I have a name—Sunflower!* And I know it's for me, and I know without a doubt that every time I turn my face toward the Son, I am beautiful because I am loved, because I am warm and well-lit.

∽

Those who look to him are radiant.

—PSALM 34:5

∽

Since that day, I have seen sunflowers everywhere. From a roadside cluster noticed in the middle of deep conversation on a run in Santa Barbara; to a Volkswagen Beetle's dashboard vase in the adjacent lane of thick traffic, noticed while driving (and running late) to my cousin's wedding in Minneapolis; to the sole sunflower, tall and graceful, staring me in the face when I had the courage to take a spontaneous solo trip with my children to a remote lakeside cabin. It is my personal reassurance that He uses the beauty of His creation to achieve His purposes, and that His plan includes *me*.

And you too, by the way.

The Beholder

We, who with unveiled faces all reflect the Lord's glory,
are being transformed into his likeness.

—2 Corinthians 3:18

The verse above sums up everything we have been learning about beauty. When we begin to unveil ourselves by stripping away old layers of lies, false definitions, and misplaced values about beauty, we are able to turn a fresh face toward God, reflecting His glory through our being. The more we allow ourselves to be transformed into His likeness, the more captivating, irresistible, and breathtaking we become. And this is not the kind of beauty that is off-putting or exclusive; it is the kind of beauty that is inclusive and alluring. We can invite other women to freedom and possibility by being free and seeing the possibility in ourselves.

∽

We are not trying to please men but God, who tests our hearts.

—1 Thessalonians 2:4

∽

Remember the old cliché "Beauty is in the eye of the beholder"? I used to think that this meant the man who was meant for me would find me beautiful. I spent the majority of my years trying to please the wrong beholders! I have fretfully hung pants of every size (up and down the pregnancy and postpartum size scales) in my closet. I have messed with makeup when I should have slapped on sunscreen and gone directly outside to play. I have eaten close to nothing in an effort to play small (and let

us not forget my snack deprivation/mood issue! Yikes).
I have wasted time worrying that I wasn't pretty enough
to keep "his" attention, when I should have been enjoy-
ing the things that made me interesting to begin with. If
only in our twenties and thirties we could receive the self-
awareness possessed by women in their sixties, how much
time would we save and savor?

Maybe you know a sixty-something woman who pos-
sesses this self-awareness. The woman who makes you do
a double take, trying to figure out what the heck makes
her so lovely when she has twenty or thirty years on you.
Look again, and see that her beauty is not about the presence or absence of wrinkles or the settling of a few pounds.
When she is busy living (not striving), she considers herself pleasing and alluring to one source only—and it isn't
her adoring husband or smitten (and probably much
younger—ha!) boyfriend. Nope, it's the Almighty.

❧

The king is enthralled by your beauty.

—PSALM 45:11

❧

We must seriously consider whose heart we are trying to capture with our beauty and understand that God's heart is the only one worth pursuing in this way. The only healthy, lasting definition of beauty and the only healthy, lasting appreciation of beauty come from God. God gave us our beauty and our purpose as a gift, and the gift is meant to be returned to Him. He is the One who deserves our praise and our passion. He is the One who loves our upturned faces. When our beauty is revealed and shared in a way that is intended to glorify our Creator, we are rewarded with a peace that surpasses all understanding, a peace that stems from being rightly related to God. We are set free from striving and judging and comparing. Women are different from men; we know this! Our way of bringing more hearts to God is through the softness and beauty of our invitation, which is issued by the way we live.

Beauty is not an outward covering; it is not something to pursue relentlessly and fight for ruthlessly. Beauty is a fountain, emanating from the core of our souls and bubbling outward, overflowing. If the fountain springs from the eternal well, our beauty, like our lives, is everlasting.

The LORD does not look at the things man looks at. Man looks at the outward appearance, but the LORD looks at the heart.

—1 SAMUEL 16:7

Listen to the way God speaks to us, hear how He cherishes us, and see how He sees us: "Arise, come, my darling; my beautiful one, come with me" (Song of Songs 2:13).

C'mon, girl, let's go!

Confidence

I am embarrassed to say that for many years I confused confidence with arrogance. I thought of pride (which is a clearly marked sin) as a good thing. I thought pride meant that you had a positive opinion of yourself and that no one could or would dare take advantage of you. I considered pride a key component of success, which meant getting what you wanted out of life and not settling for anything less.

Today I can unabashedly say that I grew up blessed. My parents were (and still are) married, and we lived comfortably. I was decent-enough looking to have dates (although some of questionable quality) and smart enough to make good grades and stay out of trouble (for the most part). Instead of cultivating a spirit of gratitude from these blessings, however, I failed to appreciate them and cultivated a spirit of entitlement. I went on for years thinking that simply by good luck, good timing, or hard work, whatever I set my sights on could (and should) be mine. This strategy proved relatively successful as I graduated cum laude from college, found employment, bought a house, and worked my way up the ladder of life. When any obstacle presented itself, I would simply dig deeper, think harder, or press on with greater force. I had applied myself, and my pride, toward the notion that I could think, smile, or push my way into or out of anything. I had little regard for those lagging behind me, figuring that unsatisfactory situations were a direct result of laziness or negative thinking.

Life pushes; push back. Something is blocking the path; knock it over, leap it, or go around it. Someone disagrees; explain more slowly why you are right. A challenge ahead? Buckle down and exceed expectations. Don't know the answer? Dress the part and act like you do. If you can't find an expert, become one. When all else fails, work harder than anyone else. This became my mode of thinking and living for more than thirty years.

In his treasured book *My Utmost for His Highest*, Oswald Chambers talks about how situations that we cannot fathom or see beyond allow us to grow and be able to recognize and have compassion for people who are going through similar trials. He writes:

> Sorrow burns up a great amount of shallowness, but it does not always make a man better. Suffering either gives me my self or it destroys myself. You cannot receive your self in success, you lose your head; you cannot receive your self in monotony, you grouse. The way to find your self is in the fires of sorrow. . . . If you receive yourself in the fires of sorrow, God will make you nourishment for other people.

I had no idea of the lessons that were waiting for me around the bend. I think my audacity might have amused God for a while, much like a parent smiles when a young child puts on a "show" for dinner party guests and everyone claps to be polite but really everyone just wants to drink their wine, chitchat, and eat appetizers in peace. Somehow this is not quite as cute at thirty. I think God had finally had just about enough of my childish twirling and posturing. The time was coming for me to truly become useful.

When the demands of parenting a toddler and infant twins began to take its toll, and the efforts of carrying a decaying marriage caused me to stoop under the weight, I went to my tried-and-true methods of handling adversity and came up empty. I tried harder and pushed on and figured I could make it work by sheer effort alone. Relationships (much like potty-training children or housebreaking puppies) do not take kindly to this approach. Slowly my efforts betrayed me. I got a clear visual of my foibles in yoga class one day. I am terrible at yoga! Being a runner, my hamstrings are about as tight as guitar strings, and when I try to imitate the posture of the instructor, I look like a bad rendition of the "Teapot" song. My heels are so far off the ground in the downward dog position that I may as well be wearing stilettos. I went to the yoga class to relax, and all I could do was compare myself and chastise myself. My teacher, Gioconda, sensing my futility and dismay, leaned down and whispered to me, "You have to relax into these poses, not force yourself into them. Try to breathe." I left class that day feeling utterly convicted, knowing her words were a metaphor for too many things in my life at the time. Years later, I still have to remind myself to breathe deeply.

I could not fathom or accept any result that did not yield success. When things began to fall apart around me, instead of admitting that I was utterly spent and my methods were futile, I then went to my public relations background and used words to hide and manage damage control. Or so I thought. I deceived no one, most especially God, who was watching and waiting with hopeful expectation for me to hand over the reins.

I waited until I nearly hung myself on the reins, and finally, at the last possible second, I cried out to God, "I can't take this! A little help here?" He, like any good parent watching a child's floundering attempts from the sidelines, was more than happy to intervene. He had a little something to teach me about confidence.

The first thing I learned about confidence was that I did not possess it. What I had instead was a thin glaze of arrogance covering up a core of fear. All those years of being "a success" in the eyes of the world had left me deathly afraid of failure. Worldly success requires taking risks that go beyond the comfort zones of previous accomplishments. Spiritual success requires letting go of expectations and outcomes and allowing God to move on your behalf. I was so afraid of failure (fear of failing myself and of God failing me) that I never really found success in either sense. But I pursued it until I nearly collapsed.

When God stripped away key areas upon which my pride was founded, I was forced to look at the resulting wreckage. I saw with new eyes that I had deceived myself for so long that I had accepted many lies as truth. I had a serious interior renovation project to undertake with no luxury of temporarily moving into a rental, and it was precisely in the messy debris of that work that God ordained a major life lesson on the subject of confidence. That lesson is what I want to share with you. The way I figure it, whatever we can learn from the page is one less pit we have to experience for ourselves.

~

[God] redeemed my soul from going down to the pit, and I will live to enjoy the light.

—JOB 33:28

~

As I emerged from the pit, I began to read the Bible with a voracious appetite unlike any hunger I have ever known. And that's saying a lot. Remember, I was once pregnant with twins! Every ounce of striving that I had ever applied to getting ahead in the world, I applied to my pursuit of God and His desire for my life. I had three child-sized sets of eyes on me, watching how I handled everything, so I was motivated far beyond myself to get healthy and make things right.

I had to relearn what confidence was, starting with my heart, moving to my mind and outward to my life and relationships. The false confidence I had known previously was built upon my own abilities and my own effort. I trusted myself, but in this world, that is sorely insufficient. Every single person (and I hate to upset you if you haven't been to this place yet) will get to a place where every skill and every effort is absolutely useless. If suddenly you find a lump in your breast, your spouse says he never loved you, you get fired from your job, your child is seriously ill or injured, what then? I'll tell you what then. Every tactic you have ever employed and every skill that you have ever mastered will get you nowhere except deeper into your own misery. This is frightening, yes, but it is also a moment of sublime liberation. When you realize that you aren't perfect, never even had a chance to be, you can finally exhale and start the arduous, dignified task of learning how to be good enough.

When you get to that place, the blank page in your diary signifying profound chasms between before and after, you are in a position for life-altering change. If you turn to God in that place, you can finally admit to yourself and to God that you are not enough. In my moment like that, I cannot honestly tell you if I cried more tears of sadness or relief.

Good Enough

And how, exactly, do we learn how to be good enough? Well, from what I've shared with you so far, you can probably deduce that step one in learning to be good enough takes place the moment you let go of trying to be perfect. Chasing the impossible, fleeting notion of perfection frees us from trying to impersonate God. (This was hard for me as I am a pretty good impersonator. I can do such a good Minnesotan accent you would swear I was from Duluth. My Ross Perot isn't bad either.) There is only one perfect being, and honey, it isn't you or me. Once that is blown out the window, we can start to let in some fresh air.

~

We have different gifts, according to the grace given us.

—Romans 12:6

~

Being good enough means letting go of expectations (of ourselves and those placed upon us by others), and focusing on the areas in which we truly do have something to offer. God has given each of us unique and precious gifts. When we use these gifts for His glory, we start to become good enough by proxy. Once we realize that we are purposely limited by time and talent, we can more graciously give from what we have. Here's an example. I love to bake, and my friend Paige has a near allergic aversion to the kitchen. When something goes wrong, or someone is sick, or I simply need to calm my anxious heart (or I have PMS and want an excuse to eat dough), I start baking. And I don't stop. I give baked goods to anyone I can think of. My friends probably see me and my pans coming and start counting calories. Paige remarked one day that she wished she liked to bake, and I nearly smacked her over the head with a 9 x 13-inch pan. If she wasted one second of her precious energy and enthusiasm cloistered away in her kitchen waiting around for the timer to go off, it would be a travesty! Her gifts are best realized in the impulsive gestures of her thoughtfulness, not delivered in a pan.

Here's another one of my favorite examples. When my friend Courtney had her first child, she applied all her career talents to making a "smooth" transition into motherhood. She kept a rigid schedule, napped her son on time, planned time for grocery shopping and meal preparation, and managed to have a nice dinner prepared and the baby bathed by the time her husband, Blake, got home from work. She kept up this facade until she could handle the stress no longer. Finally, one day, she cracked. She left the house a mess, forgot to shower, never went to the grocery store, and when Blake came through the door after work she handed him the dirty baby with one hand, held a glass of wine in her other hand, and declared the house a dinner-free zone.

What did Blake do? He fell to his knees in an exaggerated "Hallelujah!" and then spun his long-lost wife into a magnificent hug. "You're back!" he declared. Courtney's gifts (aside from being a great wife, mom, and businesswoman) are her sense of humor, her sass, her fun, and her authenticity. Those gifts, of course, were the very things Blake missed when her personality went on a postpartum hiatus.

When my friend Stephanie fell in love with Mr. Wrong, she tried everything to make him Mr. Right. Her family balked, her friends and siblings shrugged, and she tried hard to smooth over all the ruffled feathers. She tried to make him palatable by blending herself into him, hoping perhaps the mixture would suffice. Of course, the relationship ended badly, as relationships always do when we aren't being our true selves. When this happened, I got the devastated phone call. She sounded terrible! I drove to her house as quickly as I could, walked in, and couldn't find her anywhere. I was worried. Then I spotted her; my dramatic and vivacious friend, who had been playing quiet and demure for many months, was seated on the back patio wearing a white bathrobe and huge black sunglasses, with her newly dyed hair coiled in a bath-towel turban. She had a long, brown cigarette in one hand and gestured grandly to the two filled champagne glasses on the table in front of her. What I thought was a wake was turning into a celebration! Although her heart was broken, I saw the real Steph again, in all her drama and fanfare, and I knew she was going to be fine. Were things great? No. But they were good enough.

When we try to be and do the things that are outside our true selves, we turn into strivers. Strivers are people who endlessly struggle for perfection and end up with far less than good enough. Good enough is like being able to stop eating before you are bloated, or stop betting when you are ahead, or coming in from the sun before you are burned. A nice meal, a little cash, and a slight suntan are all good things. Good enough, in fact. But heartburn, poverty, and skin cancer? Well, not so much. Good enough means being able to accept who and where we are with grace and gratitude and being content with ourselves as works in progress. Being good enough ensures possessing enough humility that God is pleased. We know we can't make it on our own or by using our old methods, so we go to the Source.

In this way, the more we go to God and experience the steadfastness of His promises, our confidence builds. Not confidence in ourselves, but confidence in an almighty God. See the difference? When I let go of my old ways and turned my empty palms up to God, I could imagine His voice on high: "There you go, sweetheart. Finally, after all this time, you can be useful to Me."

~

You created my inmost being; you knit me together in my mother's womb.

—Psalm 139:13

~

It was precisely at that moment, for the first time in my life, that I understood true confidence. Confidence is not about who you are; it's about whose you are. It's not about what you have; it's about who has you. It's not about what you know; it's about who knows you. It's not about what you can do; it's about what He can do in and through you. The catalyst is not effort or good fortune. The catalyst is faith. When your confidence stems from the almighty, unchanging One, you cannot be shaken by change or circumstance. You begin to exude competence, peace, contentment, and rock-solid fortitude. Of course you do: your feet are solidly planted on the Rock.

The fruit of righteousness will be peace; the effect of righteousness will be quietness and confidence forever.

—ISAIAH 32:17

THREE

Softness

We have lost our curves.

The image of the modern-day woman is "pared down." I mean this physically, as we struggle and strive to emulate the ideal images that we are presented with in the media, so much so that now we are paying plastic surgeons to put curves back in! But I also mean "pared down" emotionally and spiritually, as we pursue the path of strength and independence by worldly standards, sacrificing the tenderness innate in every female curve of mind and soul.

God created women differently than He created men. Forget the hooey about equality as defined by "same." We were never meant to compete; we were meant to complement. It's no wonder so many women are living lives and enduring relationships marked by loneliness and lack of fulfillment. We receive so many mixed messages that we are confused! The world tells us to "be strong" and "we can do everything a man can do," but we don't take the time to really think through if we *want* to do that, if we *want* to be that way, or if we even *should*. I am in no way saying that women are physically, mentally, or spiritually inferior (not at all—please), but I am saying that we have different ways of revealing our strengths. It is our tenderness that makes us tough. It is our compassion that gives us courage. *Our strengths lie not in our edges, but in our curves.*

When I graduated from college and entered the working world, I was a naively independent and arrogant woman. I thought the more I tried, the harder I worked, the more I could make life happen for myself. I skipped from job to job and relationship to relationship in my entitled pursuit of the better deal. I scoffed at women who gave up themselves and their careers in the name of marriage and motherhood. My edge might have been helping me hack my way through the jungle, but it was also cutting a deep wound into me.

When we lose our softness, as I did in my twenties, we often have the audacity to judge or comment on things we know nothing about. How could I talk about a stay-at-home mom when I had no idea what it meant to birth or love a child? How could I speculate on women who were buried beneath their marriages until I knew the fortitude it would take to (unsuccessfully) sustain my own? As tends to happen with scoffing, I became the woman I scoffed at. I married, left my job, house, convertible, and moved to Europe and became a full-time mommy to three beautiful children.

When we force ourselves into a mold of tough strength, we break from the way God intended us to relate to men and to one another. When we cultivate an edge, we cut. Why has the female form been the object of artists for thousands of years? Why do lovers sleep like spoons? Why do we rock a baby in the crook of our arm? Love is a curve.

Relating to Men

Men and women are like the black and white curves of yin and yang shapes that form a perfect circle. When we are in proper relationship to one another, we yield a circle of strength that more easily rolls over the potholes of life. A woman's softness, or her vulnerability, is the catalyst for a man to demonstrate his wisdom and power, which in turn makes a woman feel loved and protected, which in turn makes a man feel respected and needed, which in turn makes a woman feel special and cherished, which in turn makes a man feel appreciated and irreplaceable, which in turn makes a man want to go the extra mile, which in turn makes a woman want to go the extra mile, which is what loving someone is all about in the first place.

He who loves his wife loves himself.

—EPHESIANS 5:28

You can see how easy relationship is when we relax into the beautiful design that God created for each gender. But we have a dangerous propensity to push things in another direction. Like this:

In an improperly balanced relationship, a woman feels a need to prove herself. Although she is independent enough to take care of herself, she feels compelled to promote this fact with great bravado. Doing so makes a man feel disrespected and misplaced, which makes a woman feel insecure, which makes a man feel emotionally cauterized, which makes a woman feel needy, which makes a man feel trapped, which makes a woman feel threatened, which makes a man shut down, which makes a woman nag, which causes a man to disappear, which causes a woman to feel abandoned and lonely, all of which causes the isolation that a relationship was created to dispel in the first place.

I don't know about you, but I got exhausted just typing that.

Relating to Children

I taught a character development lesson to Luke's first-grade class with another mom. On alternating Wednesdays we would spend forty-five minutes talking to the class about cultivating various character traits, handling emotions, and developing interpersonal communication skills. These forty-five minutes were always at the end of the school day and many times the class would be percolating with energy, the volume level rising as a strong case of the sillies would pervade the classroom. There were occasions when we needed to separate some children on the rug during story time, or write some names on the board for misbehaving. As the overall volume level rose, we tried unsuccessfully to regain control by raising our voices above the din.

Our inexperience was spotlighted in the drastic contrast made when Ms. Porter returned to the classroom. Even in the face of chaos, she would never raise her voice. She had a softness that exuded the confidence of unshakable authority. Her soft voice penetrated the room, and within minutes, every single child was quiet, cleaning up stations, putting up chairs, and collecting their backpacks to go home. I was in awe.

A gentle answer turns away wrath.

—Proverbs 15:1

When we compete with the chaos and noise of this world, we are diluted and drowned out. But when we use the gift that God gave us as women, and inject the softness of our feminine assertiveness, things get done! Soon enough, others around us are quieting down in order to hear what we have to say instead of our vying to be heard.

I tried this tactic at home with my own children, and it worked beautifully. I would calmly say something once, and if my instruction was not heard or heeded, I would quietly use action to enforce the consequence (put the toy up, cancel a playdate, or turn off the television). It hardly took any time at all before my children were listening to me and respecting me the way Luke's class listened to and respected their teacher. The side blessing was the peace that fell over our household when I stopped trying to compete for authority. I wasn't wielding some newfound power; I simply learned to more successfully embody the authority that I had already been given. I didn't use my edge to make this happen; I used my curve. I didn't raise my voice; I raised my expectations.

Relating to Others

Have you ever been in a crowded store at Christmastime? Or how about in a line of angry people at the airport after a canceled flight? I waited in line at LAX one afternoon, praying and listening to a woman completely tear apart a poor airline agent. She was screaming at this man as if he had personally canceled the flight by laying his body across the tarmac. Admit it, we have all been this mad at the airport, but this is a time to test our softness, not wield our edge like a machete. After the crazed woman stormed away, I took a deep breath and stepped up to the counter, determined to act differently simply in contrast to what I had just witnessed. I smiled and asked him how he was doing. He stopped completely and stared at me, silent. Then he smiled, said he'd been better, wiped the sweat off his brow, and managed to book me on another flight. Granted, I had to pay for an upgrade with enough miles to fly to Tahiti, but still, the lesson stands.

Several of my girlfriends have teetered back and forth

on the edge of sanity when their houses were under construction. One delay inevitably causes another until the entire schedule is thrown off, and costs rise as quickly as everyone's blood pressure. In a situation like this, I imagine it would be very tempting to throw a fit, spewing venom all over the architect, builder, and subcontractors. But will this move you into your house faster? And, more important, will your husband and children still want to move in with you? More likely it will only serve as confirmation that you have indeed lost your mind and your last shred of composure and dignity. Nobody really wants to help (or live with) a shrill, squawking shrew. Whenever I act like this or talk in a beastly voice to my children, my friends start making cackling crow noises at me: "Caw, caw, caw!" I usually get the message fairly quickly. The best part of being female is that when you are radiating the finest aspects of femininity, people *want* to help you make things happen.

Softness is a sweeter and more direct route to resolution, every time.

Please note that by softness I do not mean wimpiness.

Softness is not some puny form of compliance. It is speaking your truth without malice or apology. It is staking a claim without fanfare or unnecessary noise. It gets the job done with elegance. *Voilà!*

Relating to One Another

In my opinion, nowhere is the sharp edge of misguided femininity more dangerous than in our relationships with other women. We have a very ugly tendency, when we are not being aware and prayerful, to judge one another so harshly that we ruin the cooperation and camaraderie that have been God's design for women since ancient times. We were never meant to go about the difficult business of balancing work, marriage, and childrearing in a bubble! Read *The Red Tent*! We were designed to depend on other women and supply one another with support that is unique to the feminine perspective. We were created to be in community with one another. Our other relationships, with family and with men, cannot fill the spot

God intended for girlfriends. In fact, families and marriages suffer when they have to carry relational weight not intended for them.

I wrote about the phenomenon of female judgment in a blog I keep for *Runner's World* magazine:

I am not sure where or when it begins, though I see it already in the relationships at my daughters' preschool. And I can only speak of it from a female perspective, because this is all I know intimately enough to dare comment on it. Though I am quite certain that men deal with it in different ways. There is something about women that permits us to vie for a better impression of and for ourselves by belittling someone else. It rages through the gossip and social strata of adolescence and teenage years, and should by all means end when we "grow up" but somehow it does not end, it only mutates.

Think about it.

Some woman could excel in the workplace and someone else is quick to call her a witch, or worse. Someone is pretty and someone is not; they are both equally cursed. Someone is skinny and she is "obsessive"; someone is curvy and she has "let herself go." Someone has a baby and we judge between natural childbirth and an epidural. Someone breast-feeds and someone serves formula and somehow it is everybody's place to comment. Someone stays at home to take care of her kids and she is "second rate" intellectually or gets the "it must be nice" routine. Someone else works outside the home and she is "second rate" maternally or a slave to materialism. Even if we have no idea what motivates either choice or what makes it possible.

We judge if someone is snobby enough to have a nanny. We judge the poor fool who never gets out much. We judge other people's relationships, even if our own are crumbling. We judge other people's parenting, even when we are all hanging on by a thread, not an "expert" in the bunch. Someone who speaks her mind is "grating"; someone who doesn't is a "wimp." Someone with a successful husband is "a kept woman"; someone who struggles is a "poor thing." Someone who never exercises is "lazy"; someone who does take time for herself is "decadent." Someone who hides her feelings is "cold"; someone who is authentic gets picked apart. We judge who has what job, who is busier, who has more stress, who has it "rougher." Like what, like she who complains loudest is the best martyr? Or she who enjoys and is grateful is a simpleton and has no idea of the "real world"? Someone tells us bad news and we secretly rejoice that it's not us. Someone shares good news and we call her arrogant.

The funny thing is, no one ever wins because, ladies, *we are all on the same team.*

Can you imagine if we acted like it? If we treated each other like it? Because regardless of who we are, what our bank account has in it or doesn't, what we do for a living or not, if we are married or not, if we are emotionally broken or healed, if we breast-fed or not, if we eat meat or not, if our hair color is real or not, if we believe in God or not, if we are sullen and introspective or freewheeling and hilarious, there has to be a place to just BE.

After all, we were all just girls, and we are all getting old.

We were never meant to isolate one another with harshness. We were never meant to treat each other with a spirit of judgment. We have been meant to enjoy the softness of female friendships since the early days. Think of Mary and Elizabeth. Can't you see a modern-day version of their visit between lesser gals?

M: Man, am I tired. This trip was exhausting!

E: Can I take your bags? Get you a glass of wine? Here, sit.

M: I'd love a glass of wine, but the thing is, you see, I can't because . . .

E: Oh, are you on antibiotics? Are you sick? Because I can't be around germs right now.

M: No, silly. Sit down, you are not going to believe this one. (*Squeals*) Liz, I'm having a *baby*!

E: *No!* You aren't even married yet! What were you thinking? Have you told Joe yet? Cous', this is not good. . . .

M: Actually, it's not what you think. See, one night . . .

E: Spare me the sordid details. Besides, I have news of my own! You are not going to believe this! I am pregnant

too! After all these years, I just can't believe it. Zac and
I are going to have a baby!

M: Wow, honey, that *is* a surprise. I guess that explains
your mood swings lately; I thought it was *menopause*.

See? This dialogue is meant not to tarnish the holy
(please, I'm Catholic; we love Mary), but to show the difference between sacred friendships like that of the real
Mary and the real Elizabeth and the way we modern gals
distort the gift of girlfriends by poisoning them with judgment, jealousy, and ego. If there was ever a place where
the beauty of our softness is sorely missed, it is in community with one another.

If you do not have a place among women where you can
let your hair down (even if it's dirty or in desperate need of
color), speak your mind, go without makeup, laugh until
you cry, share your burdens, confess your shortcomings,
speak your dreams out loud, ask questions and handle the
answers, then you need to find such a place immediately.
Pray for the gift of godly girlfriends and then take action
to make yourself available to receive. Join a Bible study,

an exercise group, or a book club; pursue a passion; volunteer someplace that makes your heart sing; or have coffee with other moms from school. Do something to make space in your life for the relationships that will sustain you in times of plenty and in times of need. Having a life outside your home life will ensure that you keep both your sense of perspective and your sense of humor. More love just makes you more lovable, and loving.

The best way to have great curves in body and soul is to nourish yourself with good things and exercise the right muscles. If you want to use your curves instead of your edge, awareness is the first step. Decide who you want to be before the moment arises. The next time you are tempted to draw your line in the sand, ask yourself if you are drawing a curve. When you want to flip over, snuggle your pillow, glare into the darkness, and give your husband your back, think of a spoon. When you are struggling to be heard, try speaking softly so that others have to quiet themselves in order to hear you. When your child is making you crazy and you want to scream, try hugging them when you least feel like it. When you catch yourself on the verge of a judgmental statement about another woman, remember that ultimately our sisterhood is what sustains us.

Only when we realize that softness is an integral part of our beauty and our beauty is ordained as part of God's plan, will we learn to live our design.

You drench its furrows and level its ridges; you soften it with showers and bless its crops.

—PSALM 65:10

FOUR

Trust

I will never forget when my daughter Bella learned how to ride a bike. She decided (at age four, Daddy's girl!) that she was ready to learn, and she instructed us to remove the training wheels. She made a grand and ceremonious gesture of tossing them in the trash can, then we went to a track at a local middle school. There is something breathtaking and symbolic about running behind a child who is learning to ride a bike. The parent (huffing, puffing, and praying), with one hand on the back of the bike seat, helps his or her little one try to catch enough speed to attain balance. Isn't this exactly the metaphor of what we ultimately want for our children? Don't we want to be that steady hand that helps them gain the momentum they need to ride off into the distance of their own volition? Yes!

If you do the job right, at the exact moment when your child has worked up enough speed, has the balance she needs, and is grinning from ear to ear into the wind, you let go, *and she doesn't even notice.* What a stunning image of trust. You trust her to ride, and she trusts you to get her going and to let go at the appropriate time.

If she happens to fall, of course you are nearby to help dust her off and send her on her way again. The parable here is undeniable. We are the little girl on the bike and God is the watchful, winded parent. The key ingredient to success is not balance, speed, physical prowess, coordination, or maturity. The key is trust. We know God's hand is upon us; we know it's by His momentum that we pick up enough speed to stay steady. And we trust that He will not release us from His grip unless He is convinced that we are ready to ride. In the divine moment when we feel the wind in our faces, reveling in our liberty, we are always aware that He is nearby, ever watchful.

The LORD said to Moses and Aaron, "Because you did not trust in me enough to honor me as holy in the sight of the Israelites, you will not bring this community into the land I give them."

—NUMBERS 20:12

Without trust we live a limited existence. We may do decent things by decent standards and live a perfectly decent life, but because of our meager parameters and perceptions of our own abilities, we are living in a mere shadow of the bounty that God intends for us. Without trust, we can never work up the momentum to be and do great things. Oddly enough, a sign of great strength is submission.

A graceful and grace-filled woman is a submissive woman. What do I mean by that? Does this mean that I think women should be mousy and subservient, stuffing their opinions and shuffling along lamely down the road of life in bad shoes? Um, *no!* A submissive woman is one who knows that she is not in charge because there is only one boss: God Almighty. There is a beautiful release that comes when we finally yield on that one enormous point. When we stop fighting our release by vying for control, we immediately soften.

When we become malleable in the Father's hands, we are molded into the beauty of our original design. I am reminded of playing "mercy" with my brother Jon when we were kids. We would lace our fingers together and attempt to bend each other's knuckles backward until one of us couldn't stand it anymore and shouted *"Mercy!"* in order to be released. Then the winner would be smug, and the other one would typically tattletale to report the abuse. I have played "mercy" with God before too. I lost, in case you were wondering.

What he trusts [The meaning of the Hebrew for the word trusts *is uncertain] in is fragile; what he relies on is a spider's web.*

—Job 8:14

I originally titled this chapter "Submission," but then realized that submission is insufficient without a larger and more important component of spiritual well-being. We can successfully submit only when we trust the hands in which we are placing our keys. In my finest and healthiest relationships, I never have to promote my own agenda, watch my back, or vie for position *because the people who love me most are doing this for me.* And I am doing it for them. Building trust with God is accomplished in much the same way that we learn to trust people (except of course people are fallible, and God is not). Trust is built over time, through different seasons and experiences and memories forged together. Bit by bit we release more of ourselves into relationship with others, including God. The difference is that a relationship with God is not entirely like our other relationships, because He does not simply want a part or portion of us. He wants all of us. He wants the firstfruits of our time, access to all areas of our hearts, and full reign over all our decisions. His requests are not too grand; He wants nothing more than what He has already given, which is everything.

It is interesting to note that when we are in right relationship with God in this way, all our other relationships are forced into proper positioning and perspective. It isn't normal or healthy for another person to have full reign over us. When we have allocated that position to God alone, there isn't room for anyone else to take up more than their good and godly share.

~

[God] answered their prayers, because they trusted in him.

—1 Chronicles 5:20

~

We know we desire a deeply trusting relationship with God. We want to trust Him implicitly and without question, and we want Him to trust us too. We want Him to consider us worthy of promotion in terms of task and territory. So how do we do this?

Time

Look back to childhood friendships and how much time was spent in the pursuit of nothing, from lazy Saturday afternoons looking for things to do, to hanging out after school at each other's houses, to the idle blur of summer vacation. If we're lucky, some of the friendships we built during those years when we had more plentiful free time are the same relationships we treasure and rely on today. It gets harder to build relationships of this depth and with this level of understanding when we get older because we are so much busier. Busyness becomes our excuse for the lack of priority we place on our friendships. We mistakenly think we are too old to need or deserve such luxury.

The same principle is applied in our relationships with our children. I have heard it said that children spell love T-I-M-E. In my opinion, too much has been made of the term "quality time" (affectionately known as QT). I think QT is a term people mistakenly use when they are too busy to spend RT (Regular Time). Loving our kids with the QT approach is like loving our God on Sunday. There is nothing wrong with QT, a little one-on-one, or taking time out for someone, as long as it's in addition to RT, not in lieu of it.

No relationship grows (even those we consider to be solidly in place) without both parties devoting the time to continuously and deeply know each other. I am suspicious of any relationship that springs out of nowhere and takes up an inappropriate or unearned immediate high status. My friends and I joke that these are "LensCrafters" friendships, with the tagline "Quality relationships in just under an hour!" Lasting relationships have appropriate levels of shared trust based on time-tested, intimate knowledge of the other person. It takes time to know how someone reacts in joyful or desperate situations. It takes real-life circumstances to know whom we can rely on in an instant, and who will not leave our side when the chips are down. This is probably why my friends and I care so much about running together. The time spent training, early morning hours running side by side, is time devoted to the knowledge of one another. It takes a bit of time to get caught up (and this is the typical amount of time we allocate to "connecting" with our friends over lunch or coffee, then we part ways and wonder why we feel vaguely dissatisfied), and after we get caught up on what we have been up to, we can connect more deeply on the level of who we are. Relationship resides here.

People often describe their spiritual journey as "walking

with God." I used to wonder about that when I was younger and more literal, thinking of it like the famous "Footprints" poem. Now I understand it as the perfect analogy of our journey. As a runner, I can clearly understand that walking is slower and more deliberate, with more time available to change course and check out the scenery along the way. We have more breath for conversation. And it's not a race; after all, we all are trying to get to the same place, taking as many people with us as we can while we walk along.

Let the morning bring me word of your unfailing love, for I have put my trust in you. Show me the way I should go, for to you I lift up my soul.

—Psalm 143:8

Time spent getting to know God means walking along with Him; asking Him to illuminate the route and not racing ahead of what's been lit. It means spending time in

His Word, getting to know His spotless character and the countless examples of His unfailing love illustrated in His ironclad promises. It means praying, talking, sharing all the details of life and all the inner workings of our hearts. He knows it all already, but He enjoys the intimacy of the conversation. And like any balanced relationship, we can't always be the one talking. We have to make time to listen, to come before the Lord and get quiet. Not just by shutting our mouths (sometimes mine requires duct tape), but by silencing the noise of our thoughts and the rush of our emotions. God has no need to compete with the clamor and frantic energy of the world; instead He drops his voice to a whisper and waits for us to get still enough to hear Him.

There is a car wash in Austin called the Finish Line. I usually go there once a week because the neat freak in me is highly unsettled when my car has kid crust and smells like Crocs. Getting a car wash is one item on a long list of errands, though I usually save it for last. Want to know why? Because at the Finish Line there is a massage chair and while you are waiting for your car to be washed, you can have ten minutes of *ahhhhh*. It's the perfect example of taking respite from the noise and busyness of the daily grind. The car wash is a loud and hectic place; people are paying at the register, the television set is blaring the horror of world news and events, men are getting their shoes shined, small children are squealing over the fish tank and whining at the candy display, people are gabbing on their cell phones, and announcements are being made when cars are finished. But sister, when I kneel on that squishy chair and stick my face into that cradle and that perfect stranger starts rubbing my neck and shoulders, the din quiets to a blissful hum and, finally, silence. I have escaped for ten minutes, fifteen if I tip heavy. And I am a better woman for it.

After the wind there was an earthquake, but the LORD was not in the earthquake. After the earthquake came a fire, but the LORD was not in the fire. And after the fire came a gentle whisper.

—1 KINGS 19:11–12

Let's make sure we are creating the quiet and making the time to listen.

Testing

*O Sovereign L*ORD*, you are God! Your words are trustworthy, and you have promised these good things to your servant.*

—2 SAMUEL 7:28

There is one surefire way to build trust with God. Scour His Word for His promises and put them to the test! When you come up against a situation or circumstance beyond your own ability, instead of getting frightened or frustrated or calling everyone you know, try getting quiet.

Open the Bible and open your heart, and start looking. The answer is already there; you just have to find it. Ask God to direct you and lure you into the secret passages He has in mind for you. Start a journal and copy His responses to your seeking thoughts and your questions. And later, don't forget to write down exactly how He worked things out because you won't believe it if you don't see the result and the promise side by side. Then praise Him, lavishly and eloquently. Write this part down too! Gratitude is a key part of the revelation and the celebration!

The LORD is my strength and my shield; my heart trusts in him, and I am helped. My heart leaps for joy and I will give thanks to him in song.

—PSALM 28:7

As your confidence, collective wisdom, and maturity grow, it's very likely God will test you too. Hold His commands close to your heart; meditate on His words and precepts; spend time hanging out in Proverbs and making notes for your life. Be prepared for new challenges and opportunities that are bigger than your ability and beyond your training. This is going to be new ground for you, and it's going to tweak your nerves, especially if you forget that you asked for it! A life of growth is the kind of life we want, especially when growth is leading us in the direction of God. Keep your composure and hold fast to your trust in God. He will empower you. As your trust grows, so will your assignments. You might want to be writing this stuff down. Sometimes I realize later that God spoke to me in my journal, answering the very questions I was so busy asking.

Teach me knowledge and good judgment, for I believe in your commands.

—PSALM 119:66

Training

When we want to improve in any area, what do we have to do? Practice! Trying new things, approaching challenges, and employing new modes of thinking can seem very daunting at first. If we look at areas of desired improvement in their entirety, they seem so impossible that we are tempted to quit before we embark on the challenge. It helps to break challenges down into more attainable pieces. Let's take skiing, for example. You should know that I have become a total chicken since I had children. It's like I look at every adventure through a filter of potential doom, wondering how I would take care of my children if I got injured or worse. I'm working on this, but still . . . when I get off the chairlift and look down the snowy mountain, my heart is in my throat, and I wish I had stuck to my comfort zone—which means drinking a hot toddy by the fire in the lodge, where I belong. I no longer bomb down the mountain, skis parallel, poles back, crouched low for extra speed. Nope. I ski "pizza-style," with my skis in a pie-shaped wedge, and I traverse the descent by working my way side-to-side down the mountain. That way, I break the scary slope down into workable sections. *Then* I go to the lodge.

If we need to lose twenty pounds, we can't easily fathom that, but we can pass on dessert tonight at dinner. If we need to get out of debt, we can start on our next errand by buying only what is on our list and nothing else. If we need to rebuild a broken relationship, it won't heal overnight, but today we can be content with offering a gesture of kindness.

Our faith training is just like that. God's training meets us exactly where we are, which is unique to everyone. We can't look at the insurmountable task of working out our salvation and trusting God as a whole, or we will choke. We have to break it down, walk it out, take our lessons, and practice our skills in more feasible portions. Have you ever looked at a section of Scripture that you have read countless times over the years and had the experience of the words leaping off the page at you, brilliantly illuminated and perfectly suited to the current crisis in your life? I know I have. And I have shaken my head, wondering how I could have been so obtuse as to miss the point for so long. I didn't understand the passage before because I wasn't ready for it yet! The wisdom was there all along, but the difference was the understanding unlocked in me. This explains why we can so beautifully inspire and assist others who are walking a portion of the path we have already traversed.

The building up of trust, the cornerstone for a strong faith life, is accomplished in us over time. As we are ready for each new lesson, we are given opportunities to discover and work it out. I love the saying that describes how when we pray for patience, God gives us a frustrating situation. When we pray for courage, God gives us a calamity. When we pray for love, God gives us Himself.

When we pray for greater trust, God is going to give us divinely appointed and properly timed circumstances to step out in faith. We have to act on that trust before we are completely certain that it is in place, and only in this way will we have the courage to grow. Patrick Overton says this perfectly:

When you walk to the edge of all the light you have and take that first step into the darkness of the unknown, you must believe that one of two things will happen: There will be something solid for you to stand upon, or you will be taught how to fly.

As we practice our faith, over and over, year after year, it becomes less scary to trust and let go. It becomes abundantly clear that we are called to live as submissive women, trusting our heavenly Father to care for us and guide us in every way.

Trust in the LORD with all your heart and lean not on your own understanding; in all your ways acknowledge him, and he will make your paths straight.

—PROVERBS 3:5

FIVE

Truth

I had a very serious altercation with truth this past December.

It came in the form of my eight-year-old son, Luke, and his very pointed question about Santa Claus after school one day. "Mom," he asked, "is Santa Claus real? Because some kids on the playground were saying that parents actually stay up late and put presents under the tree, eat the cookies, and pretend that Santa did it. Is that right?" I hemmed and hawed, suggested we talk about it privately later (ideally not in front of his six-year-old sisters). Mostly I hoped he would forget the matter entirely, but no such luck. He persisted and eventually we sat down on my bed to have "the conversation." (Maybe this was preparation for "the birds and the bees" talk, I don't know. But I can tell you, I am not at all ready for that one.) He asked me the question again. I replied, "Luke, you really don't want me to answer that, do you? It won't be as fun." He said, "Yes, tell me the truth." I think his innocent heart was expecting me to defend the legend of Santa (that I sorely regretted perpetuating at this point, from the vantage point of the hot seat), so he could tell the playground bullies to beware of elves. I took a deep breath, and I told him the truth. "Yes, it's true. Santa is more the spirit of Christmas than a real guy in a red suit from the North Pole. I put the presents out."

Silence.

Then, fury.

"You mean *you* do that? All these *years*?! And I *believed* you? You *lied to me*!"

Ahem. Shame settles like the moon on the breast of the new-fallen snow.

"Luke, I wanted to make it special for you. All parents want Christmas to be special for their children."

"*Lies* are not special, Mom."

More silence.

Then, a flood of tears.

Oh, dear.

"Luke, do you wish I hadn't told you? I'm sorry, honey."

"No, Mom." Big sniff. "I just wish that he was real."

"I know, honey. Me too."

"Do you really take the bite out of the cookie?"

"Yep. Do you want to do it this year for your sisters?"

First smile. "Sure."

I exhale.

As evidenced by this conversation, truth can be very uncomfortable. We have pivotal moments in life when we are either asked or prompted to step up and say it or act on it. It is precisely in those moments that our character is forged and our relationships are solidified. Despite the discomfort, the truth is imperative, healing, and liberating. Either we step bravely into it and bathe in its light, or we shy away from it and spend too much of our valuable time living in shadows.

Truth is more than a status of not lying. It is an active seeking of clarity, of freedom, and of elevated thinking.

We had a silly but good example one summer day between some of my Bible study sisters. A couple of us had our kids piled into our SUVs, and we were headed out to a friend's ranch for the night. Another friend who wasn't invited called the driver of the lead car in our caravan to see if she wanted to get together. Panicking, fearful of hurting our friend's feelings, she mumbled something about doing something, basically a lie of omission, but a lie with the intent to guard feelings and preserve relationship. Soon enough, I call this same friend to tell her that a group of us are headed out to the ranch and I'd see her tomorrow and suddenly, on the phone, silence. She wasn't so much hurt that she wasn't invited to the ranch, not at all really, but she was hurt that our other friend had lied to her. She would have preferred the possible sting of the truth in love, rather than the isolation of deception, even when intended to protect.

As women, we have been socially conditioned to be pleasing and avoid making waves, so some of what we have to learn about truth is actually a process of unlearning. Sometimes making waves provides the current we need to get to the next place. Later, our Bible study discussed this as a group, and we all grew from the conversation. We learned an important lesson, and that was: however painful, friendship deepens in the fertile ground of honesty.

Each of you must put off falsehood and speak truthfully to his neighbor, for we are all members of one body.

—EPHESIANS 4:25

This is a small example, but it has larger implications. Truth is not broadly applied, like some glossy overcoat surrounding our lives. It is much more intimate, dwelling in details, and requires meticulous diligence. If we aren't actively pursuing truth, we might ease into deception by default. Just like if we don't seek humility, our human default is set to pride. Or if we don't purposefully remain focused, our default setting is distraction. Deception is sneaky, like five (okay, ten) extra pounds on the scale. If we aren't regularly weighing in, it creeps up on us.

I lived in Atlanta for a couple of years at the beginning of high school. There is a strange vine that grows there called kudzu. It grows like crazy. I'm not kidding. Like a foot a day—think "Jack and the Beanstalk." Once it creeps onto your tree or fence, if you don't kill it right away, it will overtake your entire property. Any deception, even a subtle omission or the telling of a tiny white lie, is like planting a kudzu seed in the garden of your heart. When we aren't being vigilant and constantly measuring our thoughts, words, and behaviors, we can leave ourselves open to attack.

I do not understand what I do. For what I want to do
I do not do, but what I hate I do. . . . So I find this law
at work: When I want to do good, evil is right there
with me.

—Romans 7:15, 21

For me it is a slippery slope, like taking a side route on an unmarked path but thinking I have found a shortcut. I get sloppy. I get lazy. Then I get lost. I let one infraction of integrity, seemingly small and meaningless, slide without correction. Likely I feel the tug of the Holy Spirit on the sleeve of my heart, but I shrug it off and stay busy and distracted. But no matter how small the first departure is, I have taken the first steps into shadow-living. And the pull to the shadow-lands is strong, make no mistake about it. Our culture lures us into thinking that perception and rationalization are more important than the status of our

hearts. That is so *wrong*. And living under that belief is
no life at all. But we keep going, because tiny lies are like
snowballs rolling down a snowy hillside of thick, fresh
powder. It's sticky, and it gets bigger fast.

Do you remember the movie *Raiders of the Lost Ark*?
When Indiana Jones is racing out of some tomb, carrying
a valuable statue and trying to outrun a massive boulder
behind him? That is such a vivid picture of deception and
how we think we can outrun it, but it always catches us. It
picks up speed faster than we can run.

How do we stay in truth when the potential resides in
each of us to compromise that noble intention? Well, the
first way is that we have to recommit ourselves to our walk
with God daily, each morning, before we do anything
else. We can do that in prayer and by reading Scripture.
By doing this, we choose light over darkness while it's too
early to mess anything up! Then we face our day.

Second, we have to attune and align ourselves with
the promptings of the Spirit. This recognition is highly
personal and grows in proportion to our time and devo-
tion in our walk with God, but I can offer an illustration of

how I want to be one day. Paige is an avid horse rider. It is her great love and passion and her pathway to agelessness and freedom. She spoke to me once about the difference between a good horse and an average horse. Some of it is simply innate in the horse; the rest is built by relationship between the horse and the rider. A good horse responds to the most subtle correction, the way the rider leans, applies gentle pressure with the legs, lightly adjusts the reins, or whispers to the horse. It does not take firm yanking, spurs, whips, or hollering to make this kind of horse obey. It is a pleasure to ride, a communal experience of joy between species.

And this, my friends, is how I want my relationship to be with God. I want to hear His voice whisper to me, encouraging me to speed up or slow down, alerting me to potential danger. I want to feel His tiniest tug on my heart, keeping me on the right path. I want to obey immediately and require no further correction or harsh treatment. When He leans on me, I want to know the weight of His omnipotence intimately and act quickly to adjust to His command. I want Him to find pleasure in working with

me. I want Him to be pleased, so He wants to groom me,
nourish me, and provide shelter for me. I want that communal experience of joy between the Deity and me.

~

*You were taught, with regard to your former way of
life, to put off your old self, which is being corrupted
by its deceitful desires; to be made new in the attitude
of your minds; and to put on the new self, created to be
like God in true righteousness and holiness.*

—Ephesians 4:22–24

~

And finally, though we pursue truth in our studies, it
is an application that must be practiced to become part of
us. It is essential that we walk out and talk out our truth in
the practical moments and in our daily relationships. It is
one thing to desire truth, and another thing to pursue it.
We must have the conversations that the "old self" would

have avoided. We must take the initiative instead of waiting to be hunted down.

Truth, in terms of both biblical quest and its application in the minutiae of our lives, is the surest path in the working out of our salvation. It is not easy, and when you start digging into truth, you can see why so many Christians divert from the path. Being truthful requires heavy doses of humility and the acceptance that we are simply going to be uncomfortable. Today when I am at a cocktail party and find myself making some offhand comment, sort of like a social nod to fit in (only I know I'm lying), I can feel it! I can feel the flush creep into my cheeks, and I check out of that conversation momentarily as I am spiritually convicted.

The quickest remedy is the most immediate (and most uncomfortable): 'fessing up in the moment. I tried this recently at a birthday party for a friend. A group of women were discussing involvement in an organization, and I wanted to make chitchat and fit in, so I said I had tried to get involved but could never break in. Within seconds I knew I was such a liar! I knew I never had any desire to spend my time doing that, and it never even hit my radar screen. Committees give me a rash and meetings make me queasy. Who was I kidding? So, though my intent was good, my delivery was clumsy as I blurted out, "Sorry, I just lied to all of you. I never once tried to volunteer there, and I really have no desire to do it. Ever. I am not sure why I just lied to you either." Everyone was silent. I was trying to recall where I left my purse so I could hightail it out of there, when suddenly, miraculously, everyone burst out laughing. It was more refreshing than a wine spritzer! No matter how uncomfortable it seems, we have the scriptural truth to stand on that the truth sets us free. Once we let the light in, all the shadows dissipate.

The pursuit of truth is like a salmon's upstream journey; we are literally going against the current of modern society. Our minds are taught to question and the world tells us that truth is relative, meaning that it can change based upon circumstances, comparisons, new data, and levels of experience. This is applicable to the pursuit of knowledge perhaps, but knowledge and wisdom are not the same thing. Ultimate truth is not relative. It cannot

be rationalized or customized to fit our moods and preferences. This is why the status of our hearts is so important.
Faith resides here. When our minds fail us, when we simply are unable or unwilling to think our way into the truth
(applying knowledge), this is when we must rely on the
cultivation of our hearts (applying wisdom).

An honest answer is like a kiss on the lips.

—PROVERBS 24:26

Nowhere is this more clear than in our most intimate
relationships. Here, a small untruth becomes malig-
nant. Cells of deceit rapidly divide and mutate until we
are completely ill and our relationship is on life support.
Truth is the only transfusion that brings life to an ane-
mic relationship. Once we start lying, innocently at first,
these lies build and soon enough we ourselves don't even

remember what was true for our hearts to begin with. In losing truth, we lose ourselves, and we pay the price in the currency of relationship, our most prized possession.

Even when we hurt one another in truth, we are being more loving than when we "protect" one another with deception. How much better to tell your spouse: "Honey, I feel so disconnected from you that it's scaring me. I am so vulnerable right now to attention from anyone of the opposite sex that I feel like I am in a danger zone. Please help me. I love you, and I want to get back on track and be close to you again." Painful? Yes. Brutally miserable conversation? Yes. But preferable to being discovered by an e-mail trail revealing an emotional affair with a coworker? *Yes!* You see, the truth, no matter how ugly, is ultimately kinder and more respectful than hiding. The truth will always allow for something to work with in terms of relational repair, whereas lies leave only dust.

Wounds from a friend can be trusted, but an enemy multiplies kisses.

—PROVERBS 27:6

Jesus instructs us and warns us of this simple spiritual rule again and again. The nugget to hide in your heart to be used in any shadowy situation is from John 8:32: "Then you will know the truth, and the truth will set you free." No matter the circumstance or the complexities, the axiom is simple: Truth equals freedom; deception is bondage.

As a side note, I want to mention that although adhering to principles of truth is essential, it does not give us carte blanche to be indiscriminate with our words. As I said to begin with, we must maintain our intimate walk with God above all else so we will know our place in speaking truth, and have a holy filter to ensure our words and our motives are pure, with the intent to heal, not harm. Just like my children's responses to a birthday present they hate: "But Mom, Dora is for *babies*!" or a meal they don't find appetizing: "Mom, this is so gross, I'm gonna barf!" we want our own responses to be honest, but not brutally so. When the only dividend of sharing our feelings or opinions is pain without growth, we need to discern our motives.

When our motives are clear, and we still struggle with the "pleaser" in us, we must remember whom we are trying to please. Not our parents, not our spouses, not our friends, not our siblings, not our children, not our bosses, not our communities, not our church families. No, we have one source to answer to at the end of the day: God Almighty. For several months when I was struggling with the desire to be my authentic self and my desire to be liked by people, I kept this Scripture on my kitchen window, right in front of my face when I washed dishes, packed lunches, or talked on the phone:

No one serving as a soldier gets involved in civilian affairs—he wants to please his commanding officer.

—2 TIMOTHY 2:4

When I had moments of inner conflict, I would straighten my posture (which I always need to do, please remind me), muster my most military stance, and consider my Commanding Officer. Sometimes a simple act of obedience reminds us that everything else is simply civilian affairs. And we, my dears, are soldiers.

The LORD is near to all who call on him, to all who call on him in truth.

—PSALM 145:18

SIX

Generosity

I am lucky to be surrounded by generous women. My mom loves her family and friends with selfless abandon. Paige extravagantly makes and marks moments, remembering small details and preferences that make people feel special. Peggy sends handwritten notes and surprise packages that always touch my heart on the specific day I need her, whether we have spoken recently or not. Christi showers my children (and thereby me) with delight, by wanting to know deeply who they are and what they like. Leticia cooks meals that fill body and soul with comfort and companionship. KT prays with me over the phone, embracing my minutiae with patient and steadfast love. Jennifer asks questions with tenderness and insight and really wants to know the answers. Dawn stops by with a bottle of wine and a hug, whether I have made my need explicit or not. Katie is always where I need her, right next to me. Cassie shows up, without a lot of fanfare and gush, and offers her strength.

Who comes to mind when you think of an exceptionally generous woman? It isn't so much the gestures themselves as it is the time and selfless thinking behind them. We are hungry to give and receive of ourselves in a generous way (after all, we were created in the Father's image), but sometimes we need someone to set an example for us. This is precisely the kind of women we want to be, isn't it?

We often think of "generosity" in terms of action . . . as in the act of being generous. This might mean donating time, items, or money to a charitable cause. Or perhaps it means lending something to a friend, or even a stranger. It might mean preparing a meal for someone who is ill or someone with a new baby. Southern women think King

Ranch Chicken Casserole eases everything. Or possibly offering a place to stay for someone who is moving or in the midst of marital discord. Maybe someone has been in a car accident and needs a ride someplace, or is out of work and needs a loan or a good reference. Maybe it means babysitting for someone else's children, or quietly making an anonymous contribution so that someone else's dream has a chance of coming true. These are all magnanimous and magnificent actions, and I do not mean to negate or minimize them. However, when I refer to generosity, I am referring not to these types of actions (which are truly symptomatic, the reflex actions of a generous heart) but rather to the essence of giving itself, the spirit of the person who embodies generosity.

In order to explore this topic, we need to go deeper into the personal realm of motives. I can tell you honestly that I have given (and chosen not to give) in all kinds of ways and for all different kinds of motives. I have, in the past, rationalized some of my impure motives to make them more palatable, for me and for people who know me only in a peripheral sense. My close friends likely saw through my actions the entire time and rolled their eyes accordingly.

For example, I might have given out of a sense of duty or obligation, or because of social pressures, or to avoid being left out, singled out, or called out. I have given because I wanted to be seen as generous. I have given because I wanted to please God in order to win His favor or blessing, rather than wanting to please Him because that is what I was born to do. I have given because I was put on the spot and felt uncomfortable saying no and then later sulked or steamed. These things are all very unflattering, I realize, but I want to share them so you can feel comfortable taking a look into your own motives, knowing I am not capable of (or interested in) judging you.

I recently had a wake-up call regarding my own selfishness, and, frankly, I am still reeling in revulsion. My brother Jon was in a sledding accident and suffered a head injury. He was knocked unconscious and was taken by ambulance to a local hospital, later transferred by helicopter to a better-equipped trauma center and kept in ICU. I love Jon with a depth and ferocity that is hard to describe.

He grew up with thyroid issues, so things that are easy for most of us require extra effort on his part, in all kinds of ways. I feel protective and possessive of him, and it makes our relationship different from that of many siblings. So, when I got news of the accident, my first instinct was to hop on a plane and go to his side. But instead, I hesitated. I waited on word from the doctor, hoping for quick resolution and lightness to be restored to the situation.

The next day I planned to fly out and fly him back to Texas, but when we discovered that he would be there for an undetermined amount of time, my parents went instead of me. I thought it made the most sense since I had to take care of my own children. When I looked deeper at my motives, however, I was appalled. There was a part of me that was afraid I wouldn't be able to handle seeing him or handle the task of caring for him and being his advocate at the hospital. Another part of me worried about sitting for days in a hospital room in the frozen tundra of Minnesota in winter, going stir-crazy from lack of fresh oxygen and exercise. What if there was a snowstorm, and I couldn't get back to my own kids? Wait, my beloved brother was in intensive care, and I was thinking about that?

When I realized the extent of my selfishness, I fell on my face before God (the posture Beth Moore suggests we should employ at least once daily, and I agree. Nothing like inhaling carpet fibers and enduring forehead imprinting to restore humility and proper posture before the King) and cried. I cried for Jon, for his inability to speak, swallow, or move his right arm, and I cried for me. I cried for all the years I have been unaware of just how disgustingly selfish I really am. Am I someone who gives when it's convenient? I asked God to reveal the truth and save me. The revelation was like staring hard out the window in order to see the rain. Or passing by a new mirror (maybe with outdoor lighting) and noticing (aghast!) that you have a long chin hair. You freak out and try to pluck it, wondering how you could have been walking around with a quarter-inch hair spike on the bottom of your face, and how on earth you did not notice it before. Selfishness is just like a chin hair. It's something we notice in different light. It's ugly, it's embarrassing, and it needs to be plucked immediately upon discovery.

There is nothing like a crisis to reveal motive. I called out to God and confessed my disgust, and agreed with His purposes in healing my flawed character. He has likely been waiting over thirty years to hear this from me; our Father is such a patient soul.

A truly generous woman has motives and actions that merge seamlessly. You never have to guess or gauge her intent because she wears it openly. In fact, she is always open to inspection because she has nothing to hide. This kind of generosity goes beyond action and delves into the domain of the heart.

The Importance of "No"

Each [woman] should give what [she] has decided in [her] heart to give, not reluctantly or under compulsion, for God loves a cheerful giver.

—2 CORINTHIANS 9:7

A woman with a generous spirit is a cheerful giver. How do we manage this when we have so many demands on our time and resources? How do we not cringe when some person or organization (even our church) asks for one more thing? The essence of this question is: how do we answer, from the heart, with a resounding "Yes"?

The answer lies in our ability to answer with a heartfelt "No."

Clearly marked boundaries help us define what is our responsibility and what is not, as well as what is our desired contribution (of time, energy, resources) and what is not. We have so much tied up in our no, typically so much fear regarding how other people will handle our lack of yes. We are conditioned to think that saying yes equals being pleasant and kind, and saying no equals being disagreeable or downright hostile. Nothing could be farther from the truth!

Cultivating a sincere no is a major part of growing up into our spiritual freedom. When we say no, we are allowing for our time and talents to be freed up for God's true purposes for our lives. We are creating clear space in our heads, hearts, and on our calendars so that we have the breathing room to make good decisions about what we plan to do, now that some of the clutter has been removed.

I tried this in recent years during the holidays. In my house, my children's birthdays fall in October and November, and it seems like the start of school snowballs into fall and birthdays, which bleed into Thanksgiving and suddenly it's Christmas and New Year's and before you know it the year is done. Sound familiar? One year I started to feel the anxiety rise in early October, and for the first time it was unacceptable to me to just go with that program. While I could not change the flow of the calendar, I decided to change myself. I did less hurrying and scurrying and spent more time loving during the birthday celebrations. This worked out so well that I followed the same practice for the holidays, literally letting the invitations and requests and opportunities form a pile on my desk. Then one quiet morning while the kids were at school, I put the pile on my lap and I prayed for discernment. All I heard was one word: "*No.*" I felt the stress leave my body in one happy exhale, and I promptly RSVP'd a polite no to every single invitation. It was the best Christmas season on record. Not because we had nothing to do. We did do things, but we were able to be spontaneous and enjoy the freedom of living and choosing in an unhurried fashion. It was a big lesson for me, and a big blessing for my family.

Realizing that my "no" did not need to be accompanied by a lot of explanations, apologies, or shuffling was also a great burst of freedom; it could simply stand on its own. The only person to whom we owe an explanation is God. Beginning to learn the art of saying no empowers us for the next step toward acquiring a true spirit of generosity, and that is saying yes.

Yes!

When we have the room, freedom, and confidence to practice and own our "no," we can carefully and prayerfully decide where to place our "yes." And our yes is a powerful way of defining ourselves. Where we spend our time and how we use our talents ultimately refines our character and defines many of our relationships. This is important stuff, so let's choose wisely and lovingly. First Peter 4:8–10 explains this so well: "Above all, love each other deeply, because love covers over a multitude of sins. Offer hospitality to one another without grumbling. Each one should use whatever gift he has received to serve others, faithfully administering God's grace in its various forms."

When we get in touch with our God-given desire to give from our hearts, changes occur on a heart level. This is where the difference lies between doing generous things and being a generous person. This is the graduate program I have enrolled in, with God's help. I want to give as a reflex action and natural outpouring of a healthy and healed heart. Just as we can't serve margaritas from a cracked pitcher, we can't offer ourselves if our hearts are broken and leaking. There simply isn't enough behind the gesture to validate or sustain it.

Receiving

God knows our needs before our prayer petitions leave our lips, but He wants us to utter them anyway. Why? Because He created us to be in relationship with Him. What's the use of all the splendor He made if He has no one to share it with? In the same fashion, our God equips us mightily, but He does it in an "on-demand" sort of way. We are supplied just enough for where we are right now but not enough for us to rush on ahead without Him. The point is, again, relationship. He wants us to be reverent toward the Giver, not make an idol of the gift. We have to stay connected to the Source if we want to ensure our supply. So it stands to reason that before we have anything to give, we have to have already amply received.

If a responsible parent dies and leaves children behind, particularly young and inexperienced children, he or she is not going to have a will that dispenses an entire estate in one lump sum. This is a recipe for disaster of Vegas-sized proportion (not to mention a tax nightmare).

Better to have an inheritance that is allocated wisely, over time, in proportion to the maturity of the recipient. Our spiritual inheritance is like that. God knows we are not wise enough to handle His gifts all at once, so He spreads them out over time. He must watch how we handle what we've already been given to determine the rate at which we are able to receive His divine blessings. Things like our level of wisdom, our understanding, our challenges, our territories of influence, our material blessings, our relationships . . . these are all dispensed at His discretion. He alone knows how much we can handle at each particular phase in our lives.

"Love the Lord your God with all your heart and with all your soul and with all your mind." This is the first and greatest commandment.

—Matthew 22:37–38

In order to receive anything, we must stay connected to God. We have to pray, listen, avoid sin, repent of the sin we don't avoid, and continue to seek Him with all our hearts. As we stay connected, we grant Him access to our hearts and allow Him to freely work His wonders on all our clogs and problem areas. The joy of a softened heart, a heart that readily receives, is a heart that is now able to give with the same abandon. We can give in such a way that we don't have to be concerned with running out, because we know our Source is unlimited. Suddenly, wonderfully, it's not about us anymore. As we receive, we heal, our motives align with God's, and we are ready.

We will have become transparently, porously, fabulously generous, through and through.

~

Thanks be to God for his indescribable gift!

—2 CORINTHIANS 9:15

~

SEVEN

Forgiveness

*T*he other day I saw a sweet old woman pushing her cart through the grocery store. She crept along at turtle speed, feet shuffling, the bend in her backbone causing her to be unable to lift her gaze. I could have navigated to a speedier aisle, but instead I was humbled at how she managed to get through the simple tasks that define a day.

As I walked down the aisle I was struck by a thought (other than the fact that I need more calcium). There may be hundreds, thousands of women of all ages and degrees of bodily health and fitness who are going through life like that on the inside. Age and osteoporosis are not the only ways a woman can become bent and brittle. A woman of any age, in any situation, can become exactly like that inside by carrying around weighty burdens she was never meant to shoulder.

Burdens come in all shapes and sizes; some big ones include resentment, bitterness, anger, unconfessed sin, and despair. But there is one burden mightier and more toxic than all the others in my mind: the burden of unforgiveness.

I grant such status to this big ol' burden because it is the essential reason that God sent His Son into the world. He sent Jesus to bear the burden of our sins so that we could gain forgiveness and be restored into right relationship with God. From what I have seen so far in life, a lack of forgiveness is a root cause of destruction in relationships. A woman harboring unforgiveness can appear to age a decade beyond her years. There isn't enough Botox in the world to smooth out that situation! The poison from her heart travels her bloodstream and begins to eat at her from the inside out like a bite from one of those nasty brown recluse spiders. She cannot escape herself, so the toxicity follows her everywhere, eventually poisoning the remaining relationships in her life until she is left to travel through life like the old woman in the grocery store, her head permanently looking down. And we know where we are looking when our gaze is not on God—at ourselves, our feelings, and our circumstances. Maybe the expression "Woe is me" should be written "Whoa is me" because when we are in that place, we are certainly not going anywhere.

I can trace the times in my life I have been at a spiritual impasse back to either one of two areas: fear, which comes from pride and unbelief; or unforgiveness. The latter is caused by either a heart hardened toward another or areas of personal sin. I am often too ashamed to bring personal sins into the light and seek God's forgiveness in order to receive enough of His grace to forgive myself.

When dealing with the forgiveness of others, we have a tendency to think that forgiveness has something to do with the person who hurt us. We mistakenly believe that it is an action in the natural world that releases a person from the responsibility or consequences of their poor treatment of us. *That is not the case at all.* Now, isn't that a relief?

~

It is for freedom that Christ has set us free.

—GALATIANS 5:1

~

Forgiveness is a release for *us*. It takes place in a spiritual realm, and it involves God, who is the only Source mighty enough to move a mountain as big as the damage that has been done. Forgiveness does not remove the responsibility or consequences that belong to another person; it simply eliminates our involvement in personally seeking retribution as we turn that job back to the Master. Forgiveness does not involve the participation of the other person. There are no words or actions on their part necessary to precipitate our release, *because it has nothing to do with them!* Forgiveness is a gift from God, and when we ask for it, He supplies the gift, the grace, and the guts. We can simply let the offenders know that they have been forgiven (or just celebrate with God in a more intimate gathering) and move on. The rest of the rubble is between them and God to sort out and clean up. Meanwhile, the person who chooses the path of forgiveness has already begun to live her life in freedom, leaving that burden far behind. The minute we confess God's power over the situation or relationship is the minute that person or circumstance loses power over us.

My yoke is easy and my burden is light.

—MATTHEW 11:30

It sounds so insurmountable when we are mired in hurt, but ultimately forgiveness is simply a choice. Do we choose to hold on to darkness, or do we choose to forgive and walk into the light? Do we choose to bear an unintended load, or do we choose the yoke that is easy and light? Holding on to a grudge does not hold someone else responsible, *it simply holds us back!*

We love because he first loved us.

—1 JOHN 4:19

When we think about the grace we have in Christ, and how many times He has forgiven us, it is easier to extend that grace to someone else. Remember, we know how to love only because we have been first loved by Him, so it follows that we know how to forgive only because He has so generously forgiven.

The effects of forgiveness are immediate, inside and out. Forgiveness is a softening agent for the heart that yields a more supple, more lovely appearance on the outside as a sign of the work within. Every time we let something or someone go free, we receive the freedom for ourselves in extraordinary, overflowing proportion. It is a time-tested, guaranteed spiritual principle backed by the promise of Scripture. What is the greatest commandment of all? Matthew 22:37–39 tells us, " 'Love the Lord your God with all your heart and with all your soul and with all your mind.' This is the first and greatest commandment. And the second is like it: 'Love your neighbor as yourself.' " Tell me where unforgiveness fits in here—it doesn't. Not for your neighbor, and not for you.

So once we understand the great need for and power behind forgiveness, why do we delay? Why do we continue to shuffle along, hunched over on the inside? Why do we crack under the weight of carrying it all ourselves? Let's think about this. Pray to God to give you some insight into an area of unforgiveness in your own life. If you aren't sure where to begin, start here:

Lord, I am often blind to areas of unforgiveness within my own heart. Shine Your light on me, into the dark

recesses of my heart and help me see what's there. Help
me see how I hold other people responsible for the hurt
that You came to redeem. Help me seek the gift of Your
grace. Teach me how to let go and hand over to You what
is Yours to fix. In Jesus' name, amen.

Once you can think of an area of unforgiveness, ask yourself why you have not taken care of it already and see if any of the items on the list below resonate with you. . . .

REASONS TO HOLD A GRUDGE

- It feels good to be angry. Feeling angry is the bottleneck that keeps my other, more potent emotions at bay. Once my anger is gone, I am afraid of the flood that will follow.

- This grudge takes up so much of my time and energy, I am not sure who I will be or what I will do without it.

- You do not understand how deeply this person has hurt me. If you knew, you would understand why I cannot let it go.

- I have replayed the scenes of my (betrayal, hurt, fill in the blank) movie so many times that I know them by heart, and I don't know that there are other channels to watch.

- The idea of moving on is terrifying. At least this misery is familiar.

- This person has done nothing decent whatsoever to warrant my forgiveness. They need to pay. (*Who are you, Tony Soprano?* Not only that, but, um, remember Matthew 7:3: "Why do you look at the speck of sawdust in your brother's eye and pay no attention to the plank in your own eye?" I have banged my plank into walls and around corners enough times that I am certain I have retina damage.)

- My unforgiveness is a shield that keeps other people from knowing me or loving me, and this is my sneaky plan to stay isolated so that I cannot be hurt again.

- When I hold on to resentment, at least I have control over it. This dog isn't trained to go off-leash!

Now take a look at the reasons why you should not hold on to your unforgiveness:

REASONS TO RELEASE A GRUDGE

- When we clutch so hard to the past, our hands are not free to embrace the present, or the future.

- No matter how much someone has hurt us, they continue to hurt us again and again *until we decide to move on*.

- Holding on to a grudge is not a means of controlling someone; the person holding on to the grudge is the one still being controlled.

- Only by letting down our defenses will we be healed enough to love and be loved again.

- When we aren't busy wasting our resources on feeding a grudge, we are able to nourish new, healthy ideas that move our lives forward.

- It might feel good to be angry, but it feels infinitely better to be healed.

- It's a mandate from God. Even if we can't muster up the feelings or the heart for forgiveness, obedience requires it of us. If you can't do it for yourself, do it because God's the boss and He says so.

Of course forgiving someone is too hard for us to do alone; *we were never meant to do it by ourselves!*

~

Get rid of all bitterness, rage and anger, brawling and slander, along with every form of malice. Be kind and compassionate to one another, forgiving each other, just as in Christ God forgave you.

—EPHESIANS 4:31–32

~

When I think of releasing the weight of unforgiveness, I flash back to my son, Luke, when he was two years old and learning to swim. I would stand in the water, arms outstretched, calling to him. He, meanwhile, would stand on the edge, wearing goggles, hopping from one foot to the other, and trying to work up the nerve to jump in. I am not sure if he was afraid of sinking or getting his face wet, but after much deliberation we would count *one, two, three,* and he would finally decide to trust me. He came up safe in my arms every time, sputtering and smiling.

That is just the image we need to hold in our hearts. God is waiting, arms outstretched, ready to catch us when we are finally ready to trust Him. Freedom and forgiveness are inextricable.

C'mon, baby, it's time to jump in.

Okay, Fine; Now What?

Once you have made the whopping, life-altering choice to forgive, then what? The transaction is simple. You just ask God and voilà! It is finished. But kind of like the day you are saved, say yes to a marriage proposal, or the day you sign the papers on your home loan, what seems like a simple prayer, a simple answer, or a quick signature is really indicative of something enormous that has implications for the journey ahead.

After you forgive by using God's power, you get to walk out the process of letting go, which is a collaborative effort of God's mighty power and your hard work. Letting go isn't always as simple as opening your tightly clenched fist (although sometimes deliverance is immediate. Some people quit smoking cold turkey, others chew Nicorette for years). Sometimes letting go is a process.

It was not easy for me to let go of my ex-husband, whom I now lovingly refer to as my *wasband* because "ex" sounds so mean and crossed-out. This cracks my kids up. When we were in the midst of our yuck in 2003, my lifelong friend Peggy told me something I will never forget. She said, "You know, sweetheart, things seem rough right now, but this will pass. Let me tell you something: one day you will be sitting in church, side by side at Luke's First Communion, smiles on your faces, happy to be together. Mark my words." I wanted to mark her face at the moment, but guess what? On May 10, 2008, Luke made his First Communion. Lance and I were sitting side by side, smiling. Grace and Bella were on our laps. Our families were sitting together. Peggy, Luke's godmother, winked at me. I cried. Later that morning, ten beloved people were crowded around my kitchen table that seats four, eating brunch together.

~

He has made everything beautiful in its time.

—ECCLESIASTES 3:11

~

Letting go can mean recommitting to your forgiveness decision as many times as old thoughts of unforgiveness pop into your head. Habits take time to reverse. Letting go can mean having to choose the high road at every corner for a while (think of the GPS lady: "Make a left, up ahead"). Letting go can mean making peace with and allowances for the empty spaces formerly occupied by bitterness, ugliness, revenge plans, or regret and keeping things tidy until the Holy Spirit takes up full-time occupancy in the new digs. Letting go can mean being uncomfortable for a while. Just like a healthier body has to adjust to new nutrition or a revamped metabolism, a healthier spirit has to adjust to a new diet and cleaner alternatives too. Letting go can sometimes mean having to let go of toxic old relationships, people whose only purpose seems to be keeping your old wounds fresh. When you become new you are bound to be intimidating, or at least make some people (especially those who really don't have your best interests at heart) very suspicious and uncomfortable. When people change around unchanging people, it makes them aware of their own needs for change and it scares them. They might do everything they can to pull you backward or make you question your resolve, but remember Psalm 40:2. Let me paraphrase: God has lifted you out of the slimy pit (and our unforgiveness is exactly that—a pit), out of the mud and mire; he set your feet on a rock and gave you a firm place to stand.

So don't act like you are standing on shifting sands. Get a pedicure and plant those cute feet nice and steady, on the rock.

Just as your salvation was immediate yet you have to walk out your sanctification, the release of your forgiveness is immediate but you have to walk out your healing. I can't help but think about my daughter Bella's little pet rabbit named Jack Black. His cage is in our laundry room, and I am the lucky one who gets to clean it when it stinks so bad we can no longer stand trekking to the shoe drawer. When I clean Jack Black's cage, I lift the cover off and he is free to hop around while I dump the plastic bottom into the trash and add fresh newspaper and pine shavings. The poor sweetheart barely explores or rejoices in his freedom. Instead, the second I put the wire cage back on top of its base, he hops right back into captivity! I always chide him as I close up the cage and replace the water bottle: "Silly little bunny." Until one day it hit me. How often are we exactly like Jack Black, so familiar with our own prisons that even when we are released we hop right back in? Do we prefer the perceived comfort of the barred life of bondage? Our constructed cages aren't protecting us from the outside world; they are jailing us from true freedom. Speaking from one bunny to another, when the door has been opened, let's go! Don't even get me started on the metaphor of our hamster, Cupcake, running on her wheel. Enough.

Being new, and living a new life in Christ (see Romans 6:4) free from the burdens of resentment and the toxicity of unforgiveness, is a choice followed by a series of choices. Each choice, made with God, becomes easier and more fluid as we move farther from our old ways of darkness and forge ahead, deeper into the light.

He who was seated on the throne said, "I am making everything new!"

—Revelation 21:5

EIGHT

Courage

I keep a quote, scribbled on sticky paper, next to my desk in my office. It says:

> Courage is resistance to fear, mastery of fear—not absence of fear.

> —MARK TWAIN

I have to be honest with you (before I lose my nerve to tell the truth); I battle fear quite often. When I sit down with a blank sheet of paper or a blank computer screen and attempt to meet a writing deadline or craft a speech, I am often scared. Sometimes things just flow without much deliberation or effort. But other times I am intimidated by the pressure of my time constraints or the limitations of my present creative state. It's easy to feel small when other people are looking to you for big ideas.

The start line of any running race, particularly a marathon, is also a major showdown at high noon with *fear*. My heart is racing, my mouth is dry, and I'm sweating through my jog bra long before I have exerted any physical effort at all. Just the anticipation of the miles ahead is enough to send me into a tailspin. I have a similar feeling when older, more experienced moms start relating stories about teenagers today. I start worrying about anything and everything I could possibly be doing now to mess up my kids, worrying that we will not be able to maintain our close relationships, worrying about potential pitfalls and dangers—and my kids are only in elementary school! When I walk up to a podium set at the front of a room, adjust the microphone, glance at my speaking notes, take a deep breath, and look up and smile, I wonder if people can hear my heartbeat through the microphone.

When a situation warrants a difficult conversation, and I have prayed about it, made every attempt to avoid it, and suddenly the opportunity crystallizes in front of me (clearly a nudge from the Spirit equivalent to a red-hot branding iron), I can feel my tongue grow heavy in my mouth and my spit thicken to the consistency of pancake batter. It's not fun to be brave.

I am certain it's fear (though I joke that it's sanity, of course I joke about everything that is painful to me, a transparent coping mechanism; if I make fun of myself, I beat you to it, very healthy, ahem) that keeps me from really opening up in my dating life (if you can say that I have one, very debatable). I'm wary of repeating mistakes, misjudging, being vulnerable again, or dragging my kids through any unnecessary mess or drama. Besides, I hate the feeling of wishing I could stay home and eat pizza with my kids and watch old episodes of SpongeBob while my babysitter goes on my date. What's wrong with that picture besides everything? It seems more prudent to watch from the sidelines, to be content with my work and taking care of my kids. Though I know in my heart that God doesn't intend for me to do this life-thing by myself forever, the idea of trying again is definitely an uncomfortable one.

But courage is not often found within our comfort zones. Just like when my son, Luke, wakes in the night and complains of growing pains (and I become the masseuse, procure the Motrin, and draw a hot bath), we talk about how part of growing is learning how to deal with being uncomfortable. Last winter at a book club meeting I got to hear a local swimmer named Lynne Smith describe her English Channel swim. When one of us asked how she dealt with the brutally cold temperatures and extreme conditions, she said simply, "It's pain. You have to just quit fighting it and get used to being uncomfortable." *Quit fighting it?* Wow. How often do we fight our fear instead of simply acknowledging our discomfort and moving forward? Lynne's belief is that when you fight the discomfort, you give it more power.

There is no fear in love. But perfect love drives out fear, because fear has to do with punishment. The one who fears is not made perfect in love.

—1 JOHN 4:18

What if it's a grave misconception that the thing we fear is immobilizing us? And really it isn't the thing at all, but simply fear itself. Ponder these well-known words:

First of all, let me assert my firm belief that the only thing we have to fear is fear itself—nameless, unreasoning, unjustified terror which paralyzes needed efforts to convert retreat into advance.

—FRANKLIN D. ROOSEVELT (1882–1945);

FIRST INAUGURAL ADDRESS, MARCH 4, 1933

What if the thing we are afraid of is actually no big deal? Kind of like the children's book *There's a Nightmare in My Closet*, where at the end the monster is crying, scared of the dark, and wants to climb into bed with the little boy. How much power do we give the sobbing monster? The enemy loves fear, almost as much as he loves deception! Because when we are afraid, we are unable to do what needs to be done, for ourselves and for those who rely on us. When we are afraid, we are also vulnerable because we have separated ourselves from God. So if perfect love casts out fear, we have a spiritual clue about what to do when we are afraid: go in the direction of perfect love. We need to practice doing this in every tiny trial in ordinary time, just like it's a drill we're running or a pass we're practicing, so that when times are extraordinary, we know what to do without having to think.

An assault by fear is no less paralyzing to your soul than an intruder in your home or a mugger grabbing your purse. It is an attack. A police officer would say that to avoid being the victim of an attack, you need to make yourself a less-desirable target (things like no ponytails to grab, don't walk alone at night, lock your doors when you drive), and you need to learn self-defense on the off chance that you are chosen anyway. Self-defense classes practice the same basic techniques over and over so that when we are surprised, we make certain movements as a reflex action. Basically what we are trying to do is condition our bodies to respond to training rather than fear.

I believe that a spiritual attack—like an assault by fear—warrants the same approach. The first step is to make ourselves a less-desirable target. First Peter 5:8 tells us to "be self-controlled and alert. Your enemy the devil prowls around like a roaring lion looking for someone to devour." We want the enemy to pass us over because we are simply too much trouble to bother with. We do this by walking closely with God, by surrounding ourselves with other believers, by praying with passion and perseverance, and by marinating in God's Word. Just like having a hulk of a husband, a big dog with fangs, or an alarm system, when we are living like this, there is a chance that the enemy will prefer another, less-protected target. But sometimes the enemy chooses us precisely because we would be such a prize, and this is when we need to be ready.

I had a season when I was being disturbed at night. For several weeks in the early spring of 2003, I suffered with insomnia, fitful sleep, restlessness, and nightmares. I would wake up in a cold sweat, my skin covered in chills, looking every direction in my dark room for whatever the heck just hovered over me. It was awful. The enemy had me in his clutches, happily watching me hide under the covers, and even more happily watching how scattered and sloppy I was becoming during the day as a result of my lack of sleep. My anxiety over my sleepless hours was beginning to creep earlier and earlier into my day, as I dreaded afternoon because it led to the evening, which led to night.

Finally, one night, I hit my limit. I was at the end of my rope, sick of cringing and waiting. I was not as spiritually aware then as I am now (or perhaps as aware as you are, or as I will be next year at this time, I pray), and I can tell you that if anyone had told me about spiritual warfare I would have thought they were a total freak, even though I was living it. It was a miracle I thought to open my Bible and yet I did, and there it was, my spear:

Have I not commanded you? Be strong and courageous. Do not be terrified; do not be discouraged, for the LORD your God will be with you wherever you go.

—JOSHUA 1:9

That verse, Joshua 1:9, did more for my walk with God than any other. Because when I read it, I knew it was for me, that He heard me, that He was protecting me, and that I wasn't imagining my situation. I can cry right now just remembering that sweet moment. I felt validated and vindicated all at once; and the key was obedience. There is nothing about this Scripture that leaves any room for misinterpretation. There are no caveats or what-if statements; it's a simple command. And it was just what this weary warrior needed, to be told what to do by the almighty God. It was like when my mom would yell, "Kristin Cate Richard, you get in here this *instant!*" Okay, there is really no room to wiggle there, you just *go.* And that was the firm hand I needed, to lift me beyond my measly methods and my meager expectations. He put a spear in my hand, and though I have staggered sometimes, I haven't turned back since.

Have you ever watched *The Lord of the Rings?* I am not big on fantasy movies, but there is a scene in that movie that I have watched on a continuous loop in my mind when doubt creeps into my soul. Arwen, played by Liv Tyler, takes the ill and weakened Frodo (Elijah Wood) onto her beautiful white horse to get him help. Aragorn (Viggo Mortensen) wanted to take him, but he acknowledges that of the two, Arwen is the better rider. I love that part! So she sets off through the forest at top speed with the world's only hope, Frodo, across her lap, and before long her horse is surrounded by these creepy black horses ridden by henchmen in black, frayed underworld attire. If your pulse does not race during this scene, you are already dead. She outmaneuvers all the horses, galloping across the plain, cuts her face on a branch, keeps going, and makes it across a river.

The creepy black horses skid to a screeching halt on the other side of the riverbank because the sound of a serious current is barreling down in the distance. Arwen lifts her sword high above her head (the cut on her face makes her look even more imposing) and taunts, "If you want him, come and take him!" They try to cross, but the current sweeps them away. The image of white horses appears in the churn of the current, as though Arwen's people came to her aid. I can barely type to describe the scene because it is so awesome that I want to scream. If you haven't seen it, even if you have no desire to see the movie, just watch that scene. It depicts everything that God calls us to be; it's a parable for the modern-day woman who wants to pick up her sword and follow God.

God comes to our aid, just as Arwen's people came to hers. He doesn't always let us know beforehand when or how He will show up for us; sometimes we have to start riding first. He rewards our bravery with a stunning, cinematic, undeniably awesome conclusion.

We all have our moments when we are called to "be the better rider"; the times when we have to step up and out of our comfort zones and our usual routines. As I mentioned, giving a speech is not a cozy feeling for me. Neither is hitting the wall at mile 21 of a 26.2-mile marathon. Neither is meeting a male "friend of a friend" for a cup of coffee and making idle conversation about our lives for long enough that it's finally polite to exit. It is distinctly uncomfortable, painful even, to do the things that solicit growth. Some things we avoid because we know they aren't good for us, like smoking, sunburns, reckless driving, and staying more than three days with in-laws. This avoidance is a healthy protective mechanism. Other situations, like trying new things, setting limits with people who push our buttons, saying yes to a challenge or opportunity, or having an overdue and intimate conversation, we avoid simply because we are chicken. Brave women know the difference between a wise no and a wimpy no. The cultivation of a courageous and prayerful yes is a lofty goal for us all.

Women of courage step forward when most people

would shrink back. I don't think it has as much to do with confidence as it has to do with faith, but since the two are so tightly twisted together it's hard to tell which strand is which. Courageous women know that a God-prompted yes will always have an adequate power supply. This is why praying over our decisions is the first step to living a courageous life. When I get up in the morning, I always ask the Creator of time to ordain the next twenty-four hours of my life. I don't mean just a last-ditch prayer to cover a major financial decision, a serious issue with a child, or a major business presentation. I mean complete coverage, for those major things, sure, but more important, for all the tiny decisions that ultimately make up the character and the plot of my life story.

I want God's presence in everything. From the order of my day, to the prioritizing of my to-do list, to the extra padding of time between tasks so that I have more liberty to listen and adjust to any of God's changes to my schedule. I want Him in charge of everything. All the small and seemingly inconsequential things play a larger part in the sum of our lives than the big stuff. How we treat people, the choices we make, and the conversations we have, all of it. My friend Leticia likes to say that "life is lived in the hallways," meaning the ordinary paths between here and there, the steps we take over and over until they become almost rote. Life dwells in here. And so does courage.

We can be deceived in thinking that courage is limited to the doing of great things. As Mother Teresa so aptly said, "We can do no great things, only small things with great love." This is such a profoundly humble statement from one of the most courageous women to grace our planet in recent history. We can take regular moments and, by our presence and our attention, make them sparkle with significance. We each have a major part to play in the preaching of the gospel, and as Saint Francis said, "If necessary, use words." But by our courage, our ability to love God and one another in the face of great odds or danger, we become a living invitation to the gospel for those struggling to believe. If people whose hearts are broken, whose spirits are flagging, whose doubt is raging, can look at each of us at the appointed time and see a measure of hope, we are a mark of courage in desperate times.

What if you are someone who has plodded along through life with no major trials, no sword-raising moments of glory or despair, nothing but ordinary time? What then? First of all, you can give thanks for the blessing of ordinary times, because I can assure you that anyone who is in the midst of a season of testing reflects fondly on the kinds of moments that bore you now. Second, you can recognize that ordinary times are not times of complacency; they are crucial times of preparation. Courage is built; it is not displayed in a blazing moment of glory. It's like (Oh, no way. I'm about to make a sports analogy. God help me!) a football player who makes the touchdown catch of his career in the last ticking moments of the Super Bowl. Did that player just luck out? Was he in the right place at the right time to steal that one, sweet moment of victory? No way. That moment was the culmination of a lifetime of practice, from tossing the football in his front yard as a kid to hours upon hours of drills and laps and weight lifting as an adult. The moment it counts is when all your training and all your experience come together and you don't blow it. The vectors of *who you are* and *the test coming at you* collide midpoint and *POW!* Courage is found there. Or it isn't.

This guy's off-season is our equivalent of ordinary time. This is the time spent building relationships, with our spouses, our children, our parents, our girlfriends. These are the hours we spend in Bible study, maybe occasionally wondering if we should have maybe run some errands instead. These are the regular days we come before God in the morning, with our bed-head hair, our dragon breath, our pj's, our cup of coffee, our Bible, and our fears. The moment it's going to count is coming. And everyone wakes up without a clue on the morning of the day it comes. Whether or not we rise to meet the challenge will be determined by how seriously we have taken our preparation and our training up until this point.

You see, *courageous* is a word people use to describe other people, usually reflecting on the way they handled a certain time or situation. These people were not born brave; they have no special blessing that makes them more able. *These people are us.* We are the regular people whom other people will describe as courageous when our moment comes at us like a perfectly thrown spiral, and we catch it and run with it.

Be on your guard; stand firm in the faith; be [women] of courage; be strong. Do everything in love.

—1 Corinthians 16:13–14

NINE

Diligence

Oswald Chambers says that preparation is not suddenly accomplished; it is a process steadily maintained. Wow.

I can easily and literally apply that sentence in a physical way to my training. As a runner, you don't just run a bunch of miles, do some speed work on the track, run some hills, and presto! You are there. For one thing, bodily fitness is not some end result, a comfortable plateau where one can bask and relax after exerting effort. Shoot, if that were the case, I would still be lounging around, eating chips and queso after my first marathon back in '03. Bodily fitness is a constant commitment to health and the sustained application of energy over time. Spiritual fitness is no different. A huge reason why I love running so much is for its metaphorical implications to all areas of life.

Fitness in all areas requires diligence. We can't put off exercising and then wonder why we can no longer play with our children or grandchildren, or enjoy simple activities, without becoming breathless and tired. We can't replace books with television and then wonder why we feel so intellectually flat and inadequate when we are suddenly called to rise to an occasion or we are invited to a dinner party with interesting guests. We can't say that we are too busy to cultivate and nourish our friendships and then wonder why we are alone in our hour of need. We can't put our spouses' needs consistently in last place and then wonder why our marriages are melting. We can't put our own needs consistently in last place and then marvel at our nervous breakdowns. We can't say that we will pursue a spiritual path when "things slow down a bit" and then later wonder why a crisis leaves us utterly broken.

Things that we expect to carry us, such as our cars,

have to be maintained. You can't just forget about things like oil changes, getting gas, and keeping up with regular servicing and then expect the car to take you on a road trip or get your kids safely to school. Imagine if an airplane pilot wasn't diligent about his preflight safety checklist; would you want to be a passenger on that flight? Our faith has to carry us too, and it cannot be ignored until we suddenly recognize our need to get someplace.

Diligence, just the word alone, sounds very intimidating. It means not only making the right choice once, but sustaining right choices over the course of a lifetime. It means when we mess up, we openly and honestly own the mistake, vow to do better, and move on. Being a diligent person sets the bar very high. Is it any wonder, then, why so many people think that diligence is not a trait well-suited for them?

Being diligent can also be kind of a pain. Take for example, my skin. I have naturally mousy-colored hair (thanks, Suzanne, for keeping this sad fact on the down-low) and fair skin that burns easily and is covered with enough moles and freckles that I look like a space constellation chart from NASA. Every six months I go to the dermatologist, strip down to my undies, and stand with my arms out to my sides for a thorough once-over. When I say "once-over," I do not mean a cursory viewing. My dermatologist has my chart on a clipboard and one of the pages has the outline of a body (reminiscent of a chalk drawing at a police crime scene), and every single one of my spots is marked, along with the specific diameter, type, and color. Any changes at all are noticed, noted, and dealt with accordingly. This usually involves a numbing shot and a melon-balling, which is how I affectionately describe the process of cutting out moles for biopsy. As I said, diligence can be a pain. But so far we have caught at least three spots before they became something really nasty that starts with a "C." Likewise, diligence can keep small integrity spots from becoming full-on character carcinoma.

Vectors

My priest gave a great sermon the other day that touched precisely on this subject. He illustrated the Gospel message about the wise builder (see Luke 6:46–49) with a message about diligence. He admitted that in our humanity we are often overwhelmed by what we are trying to build, the kind of life we want to have lived when we look back over our days. He suggested that rather than compare our meager starting place with the glorious result we aim for, and freeze in the face of an effort of such magnitude, we consider our destination the way a pilot does when plotting his course. We see where we are now, and where we want to end up, and we chart our paths by degrees. Each good choice we make takes us closer to our desired destiny.

The same vector theory applies to poor choices. Poor choices (like a tiny lie, a rationalization, or a lazy effort) may seem small and inconsequential at the outset, but they too are representative of a degree. Consider the trajectory of a course that is a few degrees off at the outset, and how vast the implications are for reaching our final destination. We may think we are going to Hawaii, and end up at the South Pole. Similarly, we may think we are building a sound career, only to end up bankrupt. We may think we will have a great marriage, only to find ourselves on the brink of divorce. We may think we are in good health, yet get a doctor's report that necessitates life-altering changes. A series of inauthentic choices can lead us into living a life that feels like a total sham. In all of these cases, we then have to adjust our choices and behaviors, degree by degree, until we get back on course. How much easier to simply choose to be diligent from the outset?

Part of being diligent is a lot like simply being picky. When our standards elevate, we naturally respond by being more particular about what is, and is not, acceptable. Have you ever been out to dinner with a finicky eater? A finicky eater takes the menu apart with a very discerning eye. She immediately disregards the majority of it, because it doesn't meet her standards or is simply unsavory.

And the rest of the choices she carefully considers and asks a lot of questions. The poor waiter might be rolling his eyes as she questions him about food preparation, ingredients, what is or is not "on the side," but regardless of how he feels about her, she ends up eating the meal she wants. Granted, this can be taken to the annoying extreme like anything else, but the lesson is still sound. We should be just as picky about the things that we decide to put into our lives—our relationships, our career choices, our avenues of entertainment, our conversations, and our thoughts—as the discerning diner is about what she puts into her body. As we walk more closely with God and our standards rise, we have to, and want to, make better choices from the vast menu of life. Our health depends on it.

Steady, Girl

It's hard to be diligent when we are rushed, unrested, unfocused, and disconnected from our regular prayer time.

I find that if I start each morning in prayer, then everything else throughout the day seems to fall into place. However imperfect or frustrating, I am still able to keep my humor and my purpose intact. But watch me on a day when I have started late, have missed my time with God and am catapulted, ill prepared, into an uncertain and busy day. Without fail, these are the days that I miss the mark. I lose my patience over things I normally sail over. I am discouraged by things that I might not typically give a second thought. I say things I wish I didn't say and I do things in a sloppy and hurried manner and later wish I had taken my time and done it right. Doing it right would mean stopping the rush, taking a deep breath, and starting my day over with God at the helm. With Him, I am always equipped, even for the things that I don't see coming until they are already on my lap. Diligence requires a devoted, unbroken commitment to connection with the Lord, every morning. You wouldn't drive the kids to school in only a bra, or go to the office with stinky morning breath, would you? Okay, then don't leave the house without aligning yourself with the Almighty.

Good Students

Just like a student can't skip class and spend more time at fraternity parties than at the library and expect to get passing grades, we can't expect to pass our spiritual tests without decent study habits. Ideally these habits are instilled when we are younger, by watching our parents and our mentors as they go to God, confer with godly confidantes, and consult Scripture as they make decisions and look for answers. If we are lucky enough to be able to model those who pray through (instead of play through) life's challenges, we will have a strong basis from which to draw. If we are trying to become good students at a more advanced age, we have our work cut out for us, but all is not lost. Some of the most devoted students are older, after all, especially those who are now paying for their own costly education (ouch). It is helpful to remember that good grades are not sufficient motivation. Just like the best students in school are the ones who genuinely love to learn, our spiritual education must be born out of love and desire for God.

You diligently study the Scriptures because you think that by them you possess eternal life. These are the Scriptures that testify about me.

—John 5:39

Diligent spiritual students don't mind a little homework. Wouldn't we rather pore over Scripture in an effort to learn a lesson than brave the cleanup of an experiment gone awry? We shouldn't mind pop quizzes, when we know they are administered by the Teacher for our own good. Good study habits are essential. We need to learn how to take good notes (our journals, Bible studies, and prayer logs) and to properly prepare for tests (be rested, stay focused, don't get too anxious, allocate study time, pursue areas of weak understanding, and when in doubt, ask an expert!). Just like poor Simon Peter, who declared his loyalty without knowing where his test would come (see Luke 22:33–34), we can be sure that we too will be tested when we least expect it. That is why we simply cannot neglect our studies. Preparation must be steadily maintained, just as Oswald Chambers advised.

Lazy Jane

When I was little, I loved Shel Silverstein's book of poetry *Where the Sidewalk Ends.* Do you remember the poem in there called "Lazy Jane"? It's quite simple. Lazy Jane is thirsty, so she lies down and waits for rain. Try that in the hot depths of a Texas summer, and you will find yourself dehydrated, or worse.

I have been a lazy Jane. I have lived seasons where I have been sadly passive about my faith. I have kept God at the periphery of my life precisely when I most needed Him. Someplace inside, I was aware of my own thirst, but I wasn't wise enough or diligent enough to look for living water. Instead, I waited for it to rain. My rainstorm nearly washed me away. I don't want that for any other Janes.

Maybe if we all study, pray, and learn together, we all will be adequately motivated and prepared.

Renovations

Diligence is essential in the rebuilding of a life. When we have suffered a massive blow and life as we know it has been reduced to wreckage, we have our work cut out for us. But it is precisely at those times of greatest devastation that an opportunity for a grand renovation is at hand. If we have a divine chance to rebuild, we may as well get it right.

The men in charge of the work were diligent, and the repairs progressed under them. They rebuilt the temple of God according to its original design and reinforced it.

—2 CHRONICLES 24:13

God knows we all have made mistakes, some of them worse than others. Notice I said "some of them," not "some of us" — I am referring to mistakes, not people. But God wants all of us to repent and rebuild. He wants us to return to our original design. We are, after all, temples of His Holy Spirit. He wants to reinforce the sound construction, and He wants us to be *diligent* in our progress.

Do you not know that your body is a temple of the Holy Spirit, who is in you, whom you have received from God? You are not your own.

—1 Corinthians 6:19

An architect doesn't go into a project without plans; he doesn't just wing it, hoping the beam will hold or the roof won't cave. Building something is a large and expensive effort and mistakes are costly and time-consuming. When we have personal renovations to do, we likewise need to have a detailed plan. When I was rebuilding my life after my divorce, I did a lot of thinking and researching before I actually started construction. I thought about what kind of woman I wanted to be, what kind of mother I wanted my children to remember, what kind of relationships challenged me to improve, and what kind of work I could do that would best use the talents God gave me. I prayed, I journaled, I sought counsel from wise folks, and I pored over Scripture. For every new direction in my life, God showed me passages of His Word that confirmed or better explained His expectations for me. Each step forward felt purposeful and validating as I progressed in the direction of His choosing. Even today, years later, as I am still plugging along, I am convinced that without a sound plan, I would still be spinning my wheels, standing in the same spot, trying to get my life together.

"We both had dreams," they answered, "but there is no one to interpret them." Then Joseph said to them, "Do not interpretations belong to God? Tell me your dreams."

—Genesis 40:8

Years ago when I was planning a remodel on my house, before I ever met with the designer and architect, I prepared a folder to show them my preferences. I went through a stack of old design magazines and ripped out every picture that had something I liked. One photo might show a really great bathtub, another had a countertop I liked, and one had a light fixture that I thought was perfect. In the end, I had a stack of images with arrows and scribbled notes on them. Even though I thought I was attempting to "show" these folks what I had in mind, the pictures had an even higher purpose for me. What I was doing was essentially visualizing my dream environment. I was mentally walking through my dream house and noticing all the details. Of course, everything costs at least twice the expected amount, so I ended up with only some of the things from my dream sheet, but the exercise wasn't lost on me. Visualization is a powerful tool. It takes our dreams and makes them seem attainable, even if they are far off in the distance. A diligent woman in the midst of an overhaul has to be able to visualize the elements of her new life. If you or someone in your life is at such a crossroads, try the idea of ripping pages from magazines and making a dream collage (or folder if you aren't the crafty type). Illustrating our prayers with pictures is a beautiful exercise. And it's helpful later, as a gratitude touchstone when we are living the lives we only imagined.

When we are able to envision the life we desire, we are better equipped to align our choices with the big picture. When certain people or perspectives don't match, or if they take us off track, we know when to say no or goodbye. Diligence means active choice, not a "choice" that is really the result or default of indecision.

A diligent woman understands the implications of seemingly small choices, because these choices comprise the character that inhabits the life. Things like honesty, integrity, transparency, faithfulness, and courage are not lofty sentiments reserved for special people. These are traits that God wants us to display to all of creation as a way of glorifying Him. These traits are not bestowed; they are inhabited degree by degree, as the vector of our existence leads us home into the Promised Land.

Be diligent, then, in the small choices that make up the fullness of who you are. Like the application of sunscreen, which, applied diligently over time, protects us and preserves us (and keeps us from being melon-balled and looking like a hag), so do all the small decisions we make every day.

Be diligent in these matters; give yourself wholly to them, so that everyone may see your progress.

—1 TIMOTHY 4:15

Wisdom

Our culture doesn't talk a lot about wisdom. Sure, we value intelligence, especially as it relates to career paths and educational opportunities. We talk about things like emotional IQ, regular IQ, GPA, SAT, ACT, GMAT, LSAT, and a host of other brainy acronyms. Like most things, we look at intelligence as something to pursue, then acquire, then use to get ahead.

I can talk about these things glibly because I was (okay, am) a total nerd. I had the high grades, the shyness, the studiousness, the perpetually completed homework, all of it. I thought being able to measure myself against certain prescribed standards meant I was smart. If I am smart, I can solve problems, make things happen for myself, and live the life I want. Pretty clear, right? I mean, in today's educational system, we fire up our young kids with encouragement: study hard, do your homework, pass your tests, and then you will use your good study habits to make good grades and be well-rounded in high school so that you can get into a good college, qualify for competitive summer internships so you can get a great job that leads to great promotions and great paychecks and a great spouse and great kids and voilà! Your life will be in order and all will be well. Most of all, Mom and Dad can rest easy because it will be clear to the world that they have done a great job, the icing on the perfect cake, until the candles are lit with grandchildren!

We've got the intelligence formula down. We even make our newborns lie and drool on multicolored, texturized fabric mats to watch Baby Einstein videos just to accelerate potential smartness. We stress about the best preschools when the pregnancy-test stick is barely dry. We've got tutors for our kids before they can even differentiate subjects. Our kids have so much homework that there is barely time to play outside before dinner. Soon enough we will be taking our kids on college visits during the middle school years. But talking about wisdom is not so common. It's old-fashioned, to say the least, possibly even archaic. It looks like Yoda in a Botox world. Wisdom is off-putting, and usually used in a clichéd context like a "wise old soul," or even as a humorous semi-insult— "wiseass." (Sorry. I only say it because I've been, ahem, called one.) But it is very rare in our world today that anyone actively pursues wisdom the way we do intelligence.

Wisdom and knowledge will be given you. And I will also give you wealth, riches and honor, such as no king who was before you ever had and none after you will have.

—2 Chronicles 1:12

In the old days, wisdom was everything. Spend some time soaking up Proverbs and you will practically marinate in wisdom and its importance. Remember when Solomon was asked what was the one thing he wanted (see 1 Kings 3:5)? Not wealth or power or long life or vengeance on enemies; no, Solomon wanted only "a wise and discerning heart" (verse 12) to be better able to govern God's people and distinguish between right and wrong. By the way, God was so happy with Solomon and the fact that he did not act like a self-serving chump, He added all the other stuff as a bonus. Talk about choosing well! We could all stand to learn something from good old King Solomon.

Maybe it's not as clear to us today as it was when God spoke directly to Solomon and asked him what he wanted. But He is still asking! He waits for us in prayer to ask Him for what we want. Though oftentimes we are too busy or too noisy or too clueless to know that He cares that much; that the Father of the universe really wants to know what it is we truly want.

But if we were so bluntly asked, would we be wise enough to ask for wisdom? That is a very good question.

Humble Pie

~

To God belong wisdom and power; counsel and understanding are his.

—Job 12:13

~

Some of the smartest people in history were wise enough to know just how much they didn't know. This is part of another really great trait we must reflect on often, called humility (knowing who we are *in relation to God*). Solomon had to be quite intelligent and capable to be cast in the role of king (following his father, David) to begin with, but he was also wise enough to know that his heart needed work. All of us have hearts that need work. And this is where intelligence and wisdom diverge.

Solomon asked for a "discerning heart" (1 Kings 3:9). Notice he did not ask for a discerning mind. Read that again. He did not ask for a discerning mind; he asked for a discerning heart.

Why might this be? We can do all kinds of amazing things with our minds. We can train them to memorize and understand millions of things, including a variety of subjects, languages, theories, and subtleties. We can tie concepts together. We can draw unique conclusions. We can interpret, translate, distinguish, and revise. God has given us an amazing gift in the human mind.

But 1 Kings 4:29 says, "God gave Solomon wisdom and very great insight, and a breadth of understanding as measureless as the sand on the seashore." Notice that Solomon knew that true change does not take place in the mind. So this means when almighty God asks, we should go deep and think *big*. Be so bold as to consider acquiring wisdom at a heart-level. This is where Jesus works. These are the places we cannot get at ourselves, like the irritating itch right at the center of your back, low between your shoulder blades. This is the place that cannot heal, despite hours upon hours of therapy, unsent letters, and well-intentioned conversations. This is the addiction that will not be snuffed out, no matter how refined our determination. These are the negative voices in our heads that whisper lies and will not be silenced, no matter how hard we try to drown them out. These are the mistakes we make repeatedly, even though we know that we know better.

The difference between wisdom and intelligence is the catalyst of humility.

We have to recognize our own puniness, know our truly pathetic nature, in order to get there. We cannot chase down or acquire wisdom. We can't study for it like a test. We can't inherit it, buy it, plan for it, steal it, or demand it from another. It is as elusive as love when pursued with ravenous need. There is only one way to acquire wisdom, and it is the same way we acquire salvation. I'll give you a hint: it has something to do with good manners. That's right. We recognize our need (again, humility), and we politely *ask* the Creator of the universe. And then we wait. Wisdom is not usually bestowed all at once (except maybe for Solomon), like a big wrapped box with a bow.

God handles us as gently as He handles nature. Too much rain and we have a flood; too much snow and we are buried under an avalanche; too much sun and we all live in a desert and have bad crow's-feet. Too much wisdom too soon and we will get into trouble or at the very least have a pride problem. He gives out doses of wisdom, like treasures, in proportion to our humility, our need, and our ability to glorify Him with the application. Wisdom is useless if not applied.

Use It or Lose It

∽

As the heavens are higher than the earth, so are my ways higher than your ways and my thoughts than your thoughts.

—ISAIAH 55:9

∽

Applying intelligence and applying wisdom to a certain situation are not the same thing. Let's use finances as an example. Let's say we come upon some lean times and sit down to have one of those awesome conversations between husband, wife, and Quicken. Not fun. Applying intelligence to the situation might yield a solution of cutting down on expenses, no more trips to Target, no more hair highlights and no more mani-pedis for the foreseeable future, cutting back on babysitter hours for evening fun, adding more hours onto the work schedule, staying home for spring break, making a specific budget to be strictly adhered to for at least three to six months, and setting up a meeting with a financial planner. Seems okay, right? It probably is okay, but without also applying wisdom, it is still a reactive response created by the human mind.

Wisdom always begins with prayer, because it starts by acknowledging how much we don't know. (If we knew everything, would we be in a financial pinch or a pinch of any kind, for that matter?)

Lord, open our eyes, our ears, our minds, and our hearts
to better understand our predicament. Our thoughts are

meager and insufficient compared to Yours. Reveal to us
the flaws in our relationship with money and how we can
mature to better glorify You with our finances. Whatever
lesson You have for us, we want to learn from it. We ask for
Your wisdom, Lord, to help us remedy our circumstances
and grow beyond them in the future. We wait for further
instruction as we pray in Your name, amen.

You might receive instruction that startles you or runs counter to what makes sense to your mind.

Maybe here, God responds to this request by testing your faith. Maybe He gives you Luke 6:38: "Give, and it will be given to you. A good measure, pressed down, shaken together and running over, will be poured into your lap. For with the measure you use, it will be measured to you." So you opt for obedience, step out in faith, and you tithe or you make a generous contribution to a worthy cause when what you really feel like doing is holding tight to what you have left. Have you ever tried this, in either a financial sense or in a matter of the heart? You should. It's amazing.

Do you see the vast difference between intelligence and wisdom? A good sign that you are moving in the direction of wisdom is a vague sense of discomfort. Stepping out in faith usually isn't comfortable at first.

Let's work another example, just in case the finance one doesn't reach your heart. Let's say you feel totally bored in your marriage. Let's say you are just floating along, going through the motions, feeling no passion for your spouse or for much of anything. You notice that things are getting your attention that probably should not be. And things that deserve your attention are not getting it. You recognize your vulnerability, but you rationalize it until the day comes when you can't take it anymore. (I don't mean to sound flippant, crass, or oversimplified, but I hear every kind of story from men and women these days; this is probably what happens when you write a devotional about divorce!)

You stop long enough to realize your marriage has reached a crisis situation. You apply intelligence to the situation and you decide to: (a) file for divorce; the marriage is beyond help; (b) ask around and find a counselor to talk to; at least that way you can be perceived as having made the effort to salvage this wreck; (c) tell your spouse that the sofa has his name on it; (d) call your doctor and demand Xanax; (e) have a long, gut-wrenching heart-to-heart, even though your heart is mostly numb, broken, or disengaged; or (f) say nothing, seethe for the foreseeable future, hope for the best but expect very little.

Grim, isn't it? Even more grim to consider half of married people feel this way. But our minds allow us to see only limited options. Now, let's give wisdom a try.

We know wisdom begins with prayer, right?

Lord, clearly I should have come to You before now, and I repent. I relinquish any notion I have that I can affect this situation or solve these problems. They are bigger than we are. We need You, the ultimate Counselor, the Peacemaker, Wisdom personified, to make a grand appearance in our marriage. Your Word tells us that perfect love casts out fear, and this is good because I am scared. I am scared by this situation, and I am scared of myself. Please wrap Your healing arms around us

and show us how to love each other according to Your
standards of love. Our own standards have let us down.
Help us to push aside feelings and expectations and
resentments and simply open our hearts to Your divine
love. We need You, Lord. Come quickly. In Your name I
pray. Amen.

If only you would be altogether silent! For you, that
would be wisdom.

—Job 13:5

We pray and then we get quiet, not just our mouths
but the quivering of our spirits. It may be a challenge to
be silent until wisdom arrives. (Oh, honey, that is me so
many times!) And maybe sometime soon, in the quiet af-
termath as you sit in your debris, you feel an awakening.

You are softly reminded of Ephesians 3:20 (love it, love it!): "Now to him who is able to do immeasurably more than all we ask or imagine, according to his power that is at work within us." And little by little, discouragement begins to fade. You "may have power, together with all the saints, to grasp how wide and long and high and deep is the love of Christ, and to know this love that surpasses knowledge — that you may be filled to the measure of all the fullness of God" (Ephesians 3:18–19).

Maybe that's really what wisdom is in a nutshell, anyway, a love that surpasses knowledge. That would explain why it resides in the heart and why it is a gift from Love Himself. I don't mean for intelligence to be forsaken or its importance to be minimized, only that it be better understood to be used in conjunction with the quest for (and higher application of) wisdom. When we begin to solve matters by using our hearts, we draw from a limitless well of patience and understanding, because it is the heart that is linked to the Source. And once we are filled to the fullness of God, we forget what it was that had us all riled up in the first place.

Seems pretty wise to me.

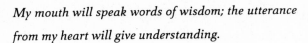

My mouth will speak words of wisdom; the utterance from my heart will give understanding.

—PSALM 49:3

ELEVEN

Authenticity

As a writer, I love words. Absolutely love them. I love to play with them, adjust them, tinker with them ever so slightly, listen to them, try them on for size, read them, write them in pen on a clean notebook page, type them as fast as my thoughts flow, hear them spoken in a resonant voice, and learn of their effect on other people. If I were forced to make a list of my top five favorite words, I have to tell you that the word *authentic* would make my list.

I like the way it sounds off the tongue, clear and authoritative, intelligent and insightful. I like what it means: genuine, true, original, reliable, and sure. I like what it signifies to me personally. In the finest moments of my life, the memories that clink and sparkle in my head like crystal glasses, I am thoroughly authentic, 100 percent present and 100 percent me. In the most dismal moments of my life, when I was lost in darkness and despair, I was most certainly living a life riddled with inauthenticity. I was a fraud, a fake, an impostor, a stunt double, a sham.

It's a word that has become a cause for me, something that shakes off my shyness and makes me want to hop up on a soapbox. It stirs my passion, gets me red-faced and pitted out, and makes me want to summon the power of all the other words I know and round them up into sentences that speak directly into the hearts of other women like arrows heated over an open flame, not to hurt, of course, but to heal. My pilgrimage for authenticity has led me to share my thoughts anywhere from coffee with a friend or stranger who is hurting, to Oprah's famous white couch in front of thousands of viewers. God took me to a dark place so that He could write His message of authenticity for me in bright lights, and it is an honor to sit and dish about one of my favorite subjects with you.

Pleasing

We are raised from the time we are little girls with the unspoken admonition to be pleasing. As girls, when we are pretty, charming, thoughtful, agreeable, well-dressed, well-mannered, and soft-spoken, we are admired and praised. This pattern becomes a prophecy as we mature. I'm not saying that those attributes aren't attractive; they do have their place as part of our well-rounded evolution of femininity. But I am saying that when we act in a way that goes against those attributes, when we are not pretty (and life can require hard work and hard times that leave no room for primping), when we speak our minds yet what we have to say isn't particularly docile or kind (however necessary), or when we have to take care of ourselves first (in order that we may have something to give), we are going against the grain. Being pleasing is sometimes necessary, as part of a reciprocal relationship or to maintain good employment. But having moments of being pleasing is very different from warping into a pleaser personality.

A pleaser daughter is one who, at any age, is still trying to please her parents. From report cards to spouse selection to career choices to parenting style, the undertone of all her decisions is colored by the opinions of the people who raised her. This is not healthy. This is not sane. This is not mature. But it's pretty common. If we aren't women like this, then we definitely have a friend like this in our inner circle. When her cell phone rings, there is an 80 percent likelihood that it's her mother, and a 100 percent likelihood that she will take the call, no matter what. God tells us in 1 Corinthians 13:11, "When I was a child, I talked like a child, I thought like a child, I reasoned like a child. When I became a man, I put childish ways behind me." We cannot be full-fledged, grown-up women if we still have relationships that cause us to regress and assume the role of a child. I am extremely close to my family, and I have worked hard to make and maintain adult-size boundaries when it would be more comfortable to go sit at the kids' table. But the hard work is worth it.

A pleaser friend is one who can't say no. A late-night tear-filled phone call or rescue mission, last-minute favors and requests, assumptions and self-absorption, are all met with some degree of cheerful (or not so cheerful) compliance. Resentment may build up on the inside, but she always shows up and takes care of things and people on the outside. What she considers to be love and loyalty may actually be counterfeited and exploited by others who seek reliance, codependency, and caretaking.

A pleaser employee is similar to a pleaser friend. She consistently works long hours without compensation or appreciation, covers for people who aren't pulling their own weight, and bites her tongue when her boss or her colleague takes credit for her creative solutions. What feels like being a martyr is really more like being a mouse.

A pleaser wife is one who somehow loses herself in the journey from courtship through commitment. She (and I mean we, because I was one too), in her pleasing desire to be the perfect wife, actually dilutes her concentration to an unrecognizable substance. When we try to be pleasing and cease speaking our minds and pursuing our passions, we become an altered version of the woman our man fell in love with. Originally, he loved our quirks and our preferences and the tangents of our personality. I understand how hard it is to hold on to these pièces d'identité when we are muddled in the haze of small children and the tides of married life, but without it we are drifting on a current that promises to carry us to a destination that we most certainly would not choose.

A pleaser mom is one who fears the loss of love from her children. She is afraid to set and enforce firm boundaries even though it is precisely those limitations that create an atmosphere of comfort and genuine respect. She equates discipline with division, and by depriving her children of the sustenance of rules she ends up missing out on the later life friendship that is the dessert of all good parents.

The common thread of all pleasers is fear. What if they knew what I was really like or what I was really thinking? What if I spoke my mind and was ridiculed or abandoned (or promoted and respected?)? Sometimes I write a piece and freak out as soon as I send it to an editor, worrying that my personality is showing too much. Like what, my personality is the unsightly equivalent of a slip, bra strap, or the top of my underwear in the ever-shrinking fashion of low-rise jeans? What if I set a limit and they hate me for it? What if I state a preference and they don't prefer it? What if I convey a belief and they don't agree? Every time one of my close friends argues a point with her husband, it escalates into a major battle and culminates with great sex. Why? Because authenticity (not arguing) is an aphrodisiac. A glimpse of your real wife, the one you pursued with reckless abandon, is a total turn-on. Real women are undeniably hot.

And not just that (though that's a lot), but when you set limits with your kids, your boss, your friend, or your parent, you suddenly become an object of interest. Just like the girl who dates and doesn't give it all away or the amazing actress who avoids the tabloid life, people want to pursue you, find out more about you, and spend more time in your good company when you have the respect for yourself to mandate respect from other people.

Being a pleaser is only good and useful in one aspect, and that is the desire to please God above all else. In that area, have at it, go for it, give it all you've got! Psalm 19:14

says, "May the words of my mouth and the meditation of my heart be *pleasing* in your sight, O Lord, my Rock and my Redeemer" (emphasis added).

Calling

Once we resolve the issue of being a pleaser, and find a healthy release for that preoccupation in our desire to please God, we are able to move on to other important aspects of authenticity.

The major identity questions "Who am I?" and "Why am I here?" are part of a deeply intimate dialogue between us and our Creator. A principal part of being our authentic selves is learning who we were created to be. We can't look for this answer in self-help books, horoscopes, therapy, a wineglass, a Magic 8 Ball, crying in our best friend's kitchen, or by asking life coaches. This biggie is reserved for the One who made us. Just like Luke and I could never create our Lego masterpieces without the almighty instruction guide that gives step-by-step, piece-by-piece illustrations; we can't even think about defining our purposes and our identities by looking anywhere besides the Source. Every other guide and guidebook will lead us to a counterfeit destination. And just like women who have face-lifts that make their eyelids look twisted into their hair and held back with a chip clip, it is quite obvious to everyone when we are not being real.

For we are God's workmanship, created in Christ Jesus to do good works, which God prepared in advance for us to do.

—EPHESIANS 2:10

God created each one of us with a unique blueprint, complete with all our preferences, quirks, desires, abilities, strengths, weaknesses, and passions. To figure out your authentic self requires a journey, in equal distance backward and forward. Who you are becoming is who you were always destined to be, before you got sidetracked by the world. The things you have loved since you were a child, the things that make you lose track of time (I have, as of now, been sitting in my office since early afternoon. I am still in my workout clothes from this morning. I have not yet showered—gross, I know. It's after seven p.m., and I just now looked at the clock, only to make my point), and the things that make you lose awareness of yourself and your self-consciousness when you do them, these are the things that lead you back to your true passion, your authentic self.

Many times, often tied into or used to rationalize our pleasing, we confuse calling with tasks and roles. We might say, "I was born to be a wife," or "I was born to be a mother." Well, of course we were. We do have a ring finger and a uterus. But our *calling*, our true designation and destination from God, is so much bigger than any definition built by relationship or assigned by a task. God loves us. He made us specifically designed to fill a certain spot in the unveiling of His kingdom. It is crucial, to God, to you, to me, and to all the rest of us, that you fully fill the place destined for you. If you skimp or abandon, we all lose. If you approximate your talent, your personality, or your beauty, we miss you. You are desperately needed. You can truly serve only by really being you.

With this in mind, we constantly pray for you, that our God may count you worthy of his calling, and that by his power he may fulfill every good purpose of yours and every act prompted by your faith.

—2 THESSALONIANS 1:11

Inhabiting

Your true self cannot be forced. It cannot be willed into existence. "Open sesame!" does not crack open the rusted, vaulted, padlocked doors of our hearts. It takes time. Just like when you move from one house to another, and you have stacks of boxes and piles of belongings, it takes time to settle in and inhabit your new digs. Becoming our true selves is a lot like that. We are spiritual beings trying to adjust to a natural world. We have to unpack one box at a time, move furniture around, line shelves, and put things away in order to make ourselves at home in our environment. As we grow up, we naturally evolve in this process, making the choices and putting forth the effort to inhabit our lives. Feeling at home in our own skin is the basis for living an authentic life.

Delight yourself in the LORD and he will give you the desires of your heart.

—PSALM 37:4

The finest things in life (love, red wine, deep friendship, a true spiritual walk, a good novel, the raising of a child) cannot be rushed. God reveals things to us only inasmuch as we can understand Him. He builds our awareness over time, valuing relationship over resolution. Your authentic self will never be a departure from what you loved from the beginning because He created you to love those things. You are good at what you are good at because He made you that way. You love what you are good at because God made you to enjoy your destiny and play your part with great aplomb. Every hint, every nuance from God, builds your character and emphasizes the angles of your personality and depth of your passion, eventually revealing your authentic self. Great sculptors don't create the art from their medium; they reveal and release it. Who is a finer sculptor than our almighty God?

What happens when you feel like a renter in your own skin? Or you feel like your identity is a wandering RV instead of a house with a firm foundation? Or you feel like you go backstage for a costume change between the acts of your life? I don't know the answer, because it is a prescription that has to be written specifically for you, no refills. But I do know the Doctor you need to call.

Taking Your Show on the Road

Speaking the truth in love, we will in all things grow up into him who is the Head, that is, Christ.

—Ephesians 4:15

Once you have spent enough time with God and His Word to start feeling like yourself again (or for the first time), you are ready to start taking your show on the road. It isn't enough to pray, read, and journal; your truth must be walked out in practical terms, in the circumstances and relationships of your everyday life. Be prepared that as you start walking out your authenticity, there might be some opposition to the real you. The primary opposition comes from the enemy of our souls, who much prefers that we live a life of approximation or quiet desperation. It scares the devil out of the devil to think that a revolution is going on, that women everywhere are becoming the women God created them to be. The enemy would much prefer us to be mousy and pliable, stuffed, squelched, and subdued. In addition, there will be other people who feel more comfortable with the old you. They might meet the new you with some speculation or resistance. The changes in you might be a sore reminder of the changes they have resisted in their own lives. They might even try to take measures to pull you back into the place and parameters where they feel more comfortable with you. But take heart, for all the discomfort of others, you will feel more at home than ever before.

What counts is a new creation.

—GALATIANS 6:15

The influence of your authentic pursuit is a blessing beyond your own heart; it shapes the hearts of those around
you. When a woman is truly free, she unlocks the doors
of hearts that surround her. Her comfort and confidence
lower drawbridges for trapped princesses everywhere! And
if you happen to be a mother, grandmother, aunt, or fortunate friend of a child, you are modeling your freedom
for them. I have struggled in this area, and every time I am
tempted to play small or let fear plot my course, I think
of my kids. I want them to grow up strong and free, and I
want them to someday look back at mental snapshots of
their mom and see a woman who wasn't afraid to be herself—a woman who loved deeply, wrote books and essays
with words directly from her heart, ran marathons, spoke
her mind no matter who was listening, laughed her head
off, and lived life with joy and reverence. I want them to
prosper in healthy relationships with friends and spouses
who solicit authenticity and encourage them to be everything they can be for God's glory. It isn't enough to talk
about an authentic life and hope our children find a way.
We have to show them by living it out before their eyes.

Your authentic self might have other opinions about your relationships, your choices, and your standards up to this point. While you may have sacrificed your identity, minimized your calling, or lost respect for yourself on some fronts, by shifting the focus back to God you can regain all that was lost, and more. Give yourself room and grace to explore and measure your old notions against the new. And give equal grace and space to your loved ones who might need to adjust or get (re)acquainted with the real you. Just as you require time to grow, others need time to grow alongside you. Authenticity begets authenticity, so be prepared for others to start being more real too. Grant the same freedom you have been given.

Anyone who really loves you wants you to be your free and authentic self. We are truly pleasing to those we love (and who love us) only when we are being ourselves. We are pleasant company when we are intent on pleasing God. Bring your best to the table. Your place card is set at the banquet; come and take your seat. We are so happy to have you.

I urge you to live a life worthy of the calling you have received.

—Ephesians 4:1

TWELVE

Freedom

$\mathcal{A}$s we move from child to eye-rolling teen, to young adult, to full-fledged woman, many of the things we learn about who we are are the result of discovering who we are not. Just as some of us learn about joy only by appreciating the absence of misery, or how others learn about gratitude only after surviving loss, or peace after riding out turbulence. Embracing and living in our freedom is a lot like that. We have to learn about limitations in order to learn (and earn) the truth about freedom.

Every teenager has some phase, however extreme or mild, of rebellion. Remember? There is a part of you at that age that wants no curfew, no questions, no expectations, no rules, and no responsibilities. Only a part of you, though. Much of the perverse pleasure of wanting those things is bucking against the authority that ensures you will have them. Talk to anyone who grew up in a household where no one cared and nothing was enforced, and they will confide to you that all they wanted was for someone to care enough about them to give them guidelines, or someone who loved them enough to have an expectation. A tiny part of us, sad to say, always remains a teenager. Next time you have a major mood swing, smile and remember this.

We may grow up (for the most part) and find ways to fit in and work with the system, but a twinge of rebellion remains. It may manifest itself as a vague, unscratchable itch, a restlessness that cannot be staved off by movement, an uneasiness that cannot be eased, a phantom desire that cannot be quieted, or an unidentified issue that is never resolved. It's like when you stand in front of the open refrigerator or pantry and stare aimlessly at the contents, knowing you are hungry for something specific but you have no idea what it is.

Questioning Authority

A certain amount of rebellion is inherent in questioning authority. Until you settle the matter of who is in charge of your life, you will constantly be butting heads with the Almighty. And since He controls time and circumstance for all eternity, you will find yourself sorely mismatched.

When you mouth off to a police officer, you might wind up arrested. Keep it up with the judge, and you might land yourself in jail. When you disrespect school rules, you end up in detention. When you backtalk a parent, you find yourself grounded. Disrespect your boss and you will probably get fired. These are basic things when we look at them with a mature perspective, but profoundly altering when we are still on fighting terms as immature advocates of our independence.

We do these same things with God. It's like a cartoon when a lion plunks a heavy paw on the mouse's tail and the mouse keeps running in place at top speed. Do you really think you can outrun the One who created your feet and the turf you are treading? It is highly irrational, but it's a common barrier to faith. If you have ever wrestled with God, you have felt the bruises and experienced the futility of it all. I remember when my own toddlers would have major meltdowns (think grand mal proportion). I once had to make a quick exodus from a local toy store, kicking open the door ninja-style and carrying my two-year-old twins, wiggling and screaming, one under each arm. It wasn't pretty. For as much as I sometimes wanted to act like I didn't know them (especially at Target or on the airplane), I knew that in order to find their peace, they needed to feel my loving authority. The best way to calm a child suffering a meltdown is to lovingly and firmly wrap yourself around them and hold them until they wear themselves out and finally relinquish themselves to the fact that you are in charge. This original friction point ultimately becomes their relief.

~

My Lord and my God!

— JOHN 20:28

~

It's the same way with us and God. After all, we are His children, and meltdowns are ageless. The more we rebel, the more firmly He holds us until we finally realize that His embrace is comfort and protection, not suffocation. When we settle the issue of authority, we are ready to begin learning about freedom.

Obedience

When our meltdown passes, and we hand the keys back over to God, we realize that obedience is not something forced upon us. It is a choice we must make freely when we are ready to progress. Interestingly enough, real freedom is found in understanding and appreciating our limits. A child (at the appropriate age) is calmed and contented to spend time in a playpen, feeling secure within its barriers. Drivers feel safe knowing that they are maneuvering their cars among people who adhere to specified traffic rules. Can you imagine driving without lanes, lights, signs, turn signals, speed limits, and railroad crossings? Rules don't ruin the exhilaration of a road trip; they simply assure you will get to your destination in one piece. Or how about when sports fans go wild, and they don't leave the stadium in an orderly manner? It isn't a party; it's a stampede. People die. When a city is under siege or catastrophe strikes and people start rioting and looting, it's not a pretty picture of freedom. It is total anarchy! It isn't fun; it's frightening. We were created to need God and His rules in order to live in peace.

I have two dogs. One is a tiny, toothless, old white (okay, usually gray) Maltese named Boone. The other is a two-year-old, 110-pound Swiss mountain dog named Mercy. With three children who like to race around the cul-de-sac, inevitably the dogs escape out the front door. Mercy used to roar through the neighborhood like a freight train, visiting all the other dogs and children and tormenting a few cats. She eventually came back home, but it scared us to death that in her puppylike exuberance she would be hit by a car. That would be a crushing blow to our family as she is a hound of enormous size and import, so I called Invisible Fence. This is a company that surrounds the perimeter of your yard with an electric barrier and outfits your dog with a collar that shocks them when they reach their limit.

There is a training program associated with the system. First the white flags are posted around your yard to give the dog an idea of its territory. They are fitted with a low-grade shock collar that beeps a warning and gives an uncomfortable twinge. You walk them around the edges of the yard on a leash for several days as they familiarize themselves with the new gig. Then the trainers come back and up the ante on the shock collar and traipse the dog around the yard, trying to get them distracted or tempted enough to breach the barrier and feel the penalty. (At this point I went inside to make coffee, not wanting to witness the learning curve.) The final training session has the full-monty collar and is off-leash. Mercy did fine until she saw Molly, the white (never gray), perfectly groomed, often-accessorized Maltese from across the street. It was too much for her; she had to go see her glamorous friend, shock or not. Of course after a brief sniff visit, Mercy was too scared to pass the flags again and return to the yard. Up went the shock level.

God is faithful; he will not let you be tempted beyond what you can bear. But when you are tempted, he will also provide a way out so that you can stand up under it.

—1 CORINTHIANS 10:13

I watched this training session from behind the glass of my front door and had to laugh. We are not so different, are we? God wants to keep us from serious pain and injury, so He designs our boundaries. He doesn't want us to be tied to a tree with no freedom, so He creates a yard for us, a safe space. He teaches us our limits, kindly, patiently, and firmly until it seems that we are with the program. Each time we get too close to the edge, His Holy Spirit gives us a beep and, if necessary, a light shock. A shock might be the warning of impending sin or a sign that our current trajectory will take us to a dangerous place if we don't reroute immediately. If we are wise, we correct ourselves and stay within our parameters. We can happily go about our business and enjoy free rein in our territory. But temptation always lurks beyond our yard, and we have pathetically short memories. We see something we think we need or want to check out and we take off after it, only to feel the shock of our own departure. Then we slink around on the outskirts of our beloved home and are too ashamed and afraid to venture back. Until our Master comes and helps us return.

Just like sweet Mercy, the quicker we learn and respond to mild correction, the sooner we can enjoy our freedom and avoid the stronger zap.

The better acquainted we are with God's expectations (His boundaries), the easier it is to meet them and stay in line. The Ten Commandments are a good place to start, though many people think the rules are so archaic that they are off the hook for any serious infractions. But in fact, the Ten Commandments are timeless. When you take out the "thous," remove the old Sunday school understanding, and apply the commandments in the context of your everyday life, you can begin to see how they very much hold relevance.

We all have the tendency to put other "gods" before our God. Things like work, money, relationships, and the opinions of others can all get in the way of true worship. Just because we don't feel tempted to carve pagan gods out of wood and put them on an altar doesn't mean we aren't vulnerable to creating idols. The prevalence of tabloid magazines is evidence enough that our society is prone to substituting substance. Just because we didn't chop anyone into small pieces and wind up on an episode of *CSI* doesn't mean we don't know how to kill. If we aren't careful with our words and actions, we can kill our loved ones' dreams, ideas, and enthusiasm. Our neglect can slowly kill our relationships.

We steal every time we diminish someone else. Making more frequent gestures to honor our parents would probably be appreciated. We commit adultery (it comes in all flavors, all of them—yuck) when we daydream about Justin Timberlake, surf bad waves on the Internet, write inappropriate e-mails, or nearly drive off the road when we pass an Abercrombie & Fitch billboard. We all could stand to be more diligent with the truth. We all are apt to push our limits, ignoring the prescription for a day of rest, and then we wonder why we are exhausted, short-tempered, and our nerves are fried. It would do us all a world of good to take one day a week to relax and be present in the company of God and our families. The Europeans have this figured out; so has Chick-fil-A.

~

This is love: that we walk in obedience to his commands.

—2 JOHN 1:6

~

The bottom line is this: in order to please God with our obedience, we have to want to understand His expectations before we can attempt to meet them. God explained all of this clearly in ancient Scripture. Then He sent Jesus to explain it all again in parables since we weren't getting it the old-fashioned way, and then He figured he may as well go ahead and send His Holy Spirit to be our full-time tutor. Evidently, the Holy Trinity really wants us to pass this class.

Freedom is found in being true to whose we are, who we are, and doing what we love to do. God would not have given us free will if He didn't appreciate the concept of freedom. He also did not create us to live lives of approximation, confinement, and misery. God's kind of freedom is not boring. Actually, it is exhilarating to move unencumbered by the bondage of sin. All the things you love to do? Who do you think made you and designed you specifically to love them? God does not intend to water down your passions; He wants to water them! He wants them to grow and be healthy and strong and used for His glory! Many of our sins are our passions that have taken a wrong turn, have been improperly named or nurtured, or have been clogged to the point of eruption. When we are living a healed life, we have holy outlets for these passions. These passions become the fuel for our creativity, our energy, our drive, and our determination. They equip us to do mighty things, things that bless us and our families and bring other people closer to God.

God wants all of you—your incredible beauty, your unique talents, your perspective, your insight, and your raging passions—and He wants you to be free.

I run in the path of your commands, for you have set my heart free.

—PSALM 119:32

Women of Grace

I love to cook. When I give myself the gift of time, I enjoy every aspect of preparing a meal. I love to sit at my kitchen island and pore over recipes and cookbooks. I like to shop for specific ingredients, taking my time and going to more than one market if necessary, indulging my pickiness. I revel in a quiet afternoon spent chopping, measuring, stirring, and baking. I like the way my table looks as it awaits my family and my friends. And I like to linger there, deep in conversation, trails of laughter winding up the staircase to where my children have been fast asleep for hours. There isn't one aspect of cooking that is unsavory to me. Well, okay, maybe the dishes.

Good cooking is not hasty or uninspired. Our spiritual evolution is like that beautiful meal. Over the course of these pages we have spent time together, considering twelve ingredients of a grace-filled woman. All of them are essential, and yet many of them complement or enhance the flavors of another. I have learned so much in my journey of creating this offering for you. I have learned about the kind of woman I want to be, but more important, I have learned about the kind of woman God created me to be. I hope you have been encouraged as well, and that God has spoken to you between the lines of these pages. We are not alone in our journey, and we are not unique in our desire to evolve in a way that pleases God. There is only so much self-improvement we can achieve; the quest is popular, but unfortunately it is short-lived and short on results. Our self-improvement is limited to just that, our selves. We can and must think bigger than that. God has things in store for us that would blow our minds.

I am going to do something in your days that you would never believe, even if someone told you.

—ACTS 13:41

I have no doubt that God will illuminate areas for growth and provide you with real-life circumstances in which to step out in faith. He continues to do this for me. I can barely keep up with what He's teaching me. In addition to being in God's good company, it is my prayer for you that you have or will find a group of women to share this journey with. These twelve traits are better explored together. I think when we are at our best, women can hone and reveal one another like nothing else. "As iron sharpens iron, so one [woman] sharpens another" (Proverbs 27:17). I have created some discussion questions following this chapter as a starting place, though please don't allow these to limit your conversation.

Take your time. Enjoy being a work in progress. Revel in the adventure. Bask in your unveiling. The more transparent we become, the more God's light can shine through us and illuminate the way for someone else. We are all unfinished, but bit by bit the glory of His likeness is being revealed. We are, after all, created to be beautiful, confident, soft, trusting, truthful, generous, forgiving, courageous, diligent, wise, authentic, and free.

It has been an honor and a pleasure to walk alongside you.

In love and faith,

Kristin

Discussion/Journal Questions

Chapter One: Beauty

1. What lies (from childhood through the present) have you believed about your beauty and your being? Write them all down.
2. What did you like to do as a child that set your heart free? What made you lose track of time? What could you not wait to do?
3. Pray and ask God to reveal how He sees you. Ask Him where your beauty lies. Take some quiet time and journal how He speaks to you.

4. If God looks at the heart instead of outward beauty, what is it about your heart that could use some freshening up?

5. As your beauty is revealed, how will this change the way you act? Will it change how you carry yourself? Or how you treat yourself and others?

Chapter Two: Confidence

1. Have you ever confused confidence with arrogance? Describe the difference now that you know better.

2. Describe how you have pursued perfection. What steps led you (or are leading you) to stop striving?

3. What are your gifts? Don't be shy or exalted; be real. If you honestly don't know, ask your best friend. How do you feel when you are using your gifts?

4. Define "good enough." Why is this concept so important?

5. Review the Scripture from Isaiah 32. Confidence is a result of righteousness and peace. Journal about a moment when you felt truly confident. What were you

doing and how were you doing it? How can you cultivate a life like that? You glorify God when you are being that woman, your true and undeniable self.

Chapter Three: Softness

1. Tell me about your edge. How have you cultivated it?
   How does it exhibit itself? Who is getting cut?
2. What is your inner relationship with authority? Do
   you struggle for power or do you effectively assume the
   power that is yours to begin with?
3. How are your relationships with other women? Do
   you have friendships that enrich and bless your life or
   are you lonely for connection? Why?
4. Do you use your edge or your curve in your relationship with your man (past or present; you can't skip the
   question)?
5. What are some ways you can start practicing using
   your curve (your softness) to be the woman God created you to be? Journal some ideas and leave space to
   go back and fill in what happened.

Chapter Four: Trust

1. Do you have an example from your life that illustrates the concept of trust (like Bella on her bike)?

2. The word *submissive* has taken a bad rap in our culture. It seems to be a virtue that goes against the grain of feminine progress. How is the word *submission* meant to be understood in this chapter, and why is it important?

3. How do the trusting relationships in your life parallel the relationship that is intended between you and God? Who has your back and how do you know?

4. Open your calendar and scan back over the past three weeks. Note your expenditure of time. How much have you reserved for God, for yourself, for your family, for your friends? Are you in balance, or what changes would you like to see? How would your friends perceive your balance?

5. Discuss QT versus RT. Do you agree with me or do you think I'm nuts?

6. Do you keep a journal where you log your spiritual life? If not, start one.

7. Can you relate to the metaphor of training? How do you train in your life and for what are you training?

8. What large mountain currently looms before you? How can you break down the journey or task ahead into more-feasible portions or sections?

9. What relationship in your life on earth most closely models the example of a trusting relationship with the Lord? Tell that person how much you love and appreciate them — today.

Chapter Five: Truth

1. Have you had a pivotal moment of truth, where you were required to step out of the shadows and speak up? If so, how did that feel and what was the reaction?

2. When have difficult words from a friend (or to a friend) offered healing that outweighed the hurt?

3. I describe deception as the creeping numbers on a scale, a kudzu vine, and the boulder chasing Indiana Jones. Can you relate to these images? How have you recognized and dealt with the insidious nature of deception in your own life?

4. What are some initiatives that you intend to make in order to remain in the light of truth?

5. How has John 8:32 spoken to you in your life experience? When has the truth liberated you?

6. Do you struggle with being a pleaser? How can 2 Timothy 2:4 help you combat this problem?

Chapter Six: Generosity

1. Who do you consider a fine example of a generous woman? What is it about her that strikes you?

2. What motives are behind your acts of generosity? Do you feel you are pure and rightly related to God or does your heart need some work?

3. What areas of your life need boundary work? Where are you having trouble saying no? Why?

4. Where is God prompting you to say yes? What's holding you back?

5. What steps can you take to stay connected to God and learn to receive His grace?

Chapter Seven: Forgiveness

1. What areas of unforgiveness are you clutching tightly? What might be causing your spiritual posture to stoop?
2. What is keeping you from letting go?
3. Envision your life without this heavy burden. What does it look like?
4. What might God have in store for you when your hands are finally free to receive?
5. How is the Holy Spirit prompting you to act on behalf of your own release? Don't be like Bella's bunny!
6. How are you going to celebrate?

Chapter Eight: Courage

1. What role does fear play in your life? What scares you? What makes you "pit out"? What turns your spit to pancake batter?
2. If courage is not found within our comfort zones, what draws you beyond yourself? How do you quit fighting

pain and grow more accustomed to being uncomfortable?

3. Have you ever been the victim of a spiritual attack? How can you go about making yourself less vulnerable in the future?

4. Joshua 1:9 is my spear. How do you combat fear with perfect love?

5. How has God come to your rescue as Arwen's people came to hers in *The Lord of the Rings*?

6. What are "the painful areas that solicit growth" that you are being called into today? In what area is God calling you to step forward when everything in you wants to shrink back?

7. How can you become a living witness of the gospel for those struggling to believe? How can you do small things with great love in your life this week? Write them down, and do them!

8. How can you manifest the attribute of courage in the happenings of your daily life? What does that look like to you? How does it feel?

Chapter Nine: Diligence

1. What areas of your life are blossoming as the result of your diligence? What areas are lagging behind?

2. How can you apply the "vector theory" when you consider small choices that can help some of your sloppy areas get back on track? Where can you begin actively making a difference today?

3. Is your daily prayer life a steady connection that keeps you constantly replenished? Is your life richly focused? If not, how can you make sure that you do first things first each morning?

4. Describe your study habits. Are you a good spiritual student?

5. Have you ever been or are you presently in the midst of personal renovations? What areas of your life are under construction? How are you taking steps to be diligent in the rebuilding of the life of your dreams? Make a dream collage or folder if you have never done a visualization exercise before. Put it someplace where you can view it regularly. If this seems like a pain, you might want to rethink your effort level a bit.

Chapter Ten: Wisdom

1. Have you placed a higher value on intelligence than on wisdom in your life? How so?

2. If you were King Solomon today and God asked you what you wanted, how might you respond?

3. Do you agree that humility is the catalyst to wisdom? Why or why not?

4. Why might wisdom be uncomfortable?

5. Illustrate with your own personal example the difference between how a situation is handled with intelligence versus wisdom.

6. If the discussion is sufficiently open, take a moment to pen a prayer for someone else in the group to spark her petition for wisdom.

7. To what circumstance in your life right now could you apply the beauty and power of Ephesians 3:20?

8. How would your life be different if you were filled to the measure of all the fullness of God?

Chapter Eleven: Authenticity

1. What does authenticity mean to you? Rate yourself on a scale from one to ten (with ten meaning living your truest life) in terms of your life and relationships reflecting who you really are.

2. Are you a pleaser? In what ways and with whom?

3. Can you trace your desire to please back to your childhood? Is it rooted in fear? If so, how?

4. Do you know who you are, and why you are here? Have you found your true calling?

5. What do you do that makes you lose track of time and inhibitions?

6. How can you align your life to reflect your desire?

7. Do you feel opposition when you act authentically?

8. Who opposes you and why?

9. How can and will you address the obstacles that are preventing you from being real?

Chapter Twelve: Freedom

1. Can you recognize areas of rebellion in your spirit? List any examples of restlessness or anxiety that might exemplify why you need to settle the issue of authority.

2. Do your boundaries need refinement? If so, which ones?

3. What areas of disobedience do you need to bring into alignment with the Master?

4. Are there any particular commandments that you need to focus on? Journal which ones and why, and how you can begin to do the work.

5. What passions of yours have been improperly named or nurtured?

6. How can these same passions be transformed with God's grace into something redeeming, your unique offering to the King?

7. Journal about the area (or areas) of your life where you would most like to enjoy freedom. What would your life look like if you were living freely in this specific area? How can you begin (pray and search Scripture if you don't know) to take steps in the pursuit of that freedom?

The child grew and became strong; he was filled with wisdom, and the *grac*

one blessing after another. —JOHN 1:16 With great power the apostles continu

—ACTS 4:33 When [Barnabas] arrived and saw the evidence of the *grace* o

11:23 To all in Rome who are loved by God and called to be saints: *grace* an

different gifts, according to the *grace* given us. —ROMANS 12:6 I have writte

God gave me. —ROMANS 15:15 Now this is our boast: Our conscience testifies

holiness and sincerity that are from God. We have done so not according to worldly

we urge you not to receive God's *grace* in vain. —2 CORINTHIANS 6:1 In the

given you. —2 CORINTHIANS 9:14 I do not set aside the *grace* of God, for if

the praise of his glorious *grace*, which he has freely given us in the One he love

—EPHESIANS 4:7 Let your conversation be always full of *grace*, seasoned wi

our Lord was poured out on me abundantly, along with the faith and love that are in C

in Christ, after you have suffered a little while, will himself restore you and make you s

and Savior Jesus Christ. To him be glory both now and forever! Amen. —2 PETER 3: